Know about prayers yourself

yourself

Uncover the Transformative Essence of Prayer

By

David J. Gouge

Copyright

Disclaimer

"Know About Prayer Yourself" is a personal exploration into the realms of prayer and self-awareness. The stories, insights, and perspectives shared are based on personal experiences and are not intended to substitute professional advice or religious guidance. The author is not responsible for any consequences arising from actions taken based on the content of this book.

This book is a conversation, a sharing of thoughts and ideas. Your interpretation of these pages is as valid as the words on them. Remember, we're all on unique journeys, and this book is just a companion on yours.

Thanks for being part of this adventure.

Warmest wishes,

David J. Gouge

About the Author

The person who put heart and emotion into the words you just read is me, David J. Gouge. For me, writing is more than just a job; it's a reflection of who I am as a dreamer, a storyteller, and an inquisitive person enduring this crazy journey called life.My passion for stories began at a young age. Books grew to be my friends, leading me into realms where anything was imaginable. As the writer of this book, my goal is to tell tales that touch you, stay with you, and perhaps even make an impression on your heart.Apart from writing, I manage several other responsibilities; I may be a

father, a traveller, a coffee lover, or a combination of all three. Every experience is a source of inspiration, and life, with all of its turns and turns, is my playground.I really think that stories have a magical power. They have this amazing power to unite us and let us feel less isolated amid the grandeur of the cosmos. Therefore, know that I'm here and incredibly glad for the opportunity to share a small portion of my world with you as you read through these pages and begin to wonder about the person behind the words.We appreciate your participation in this adventure. More adventures, stories, and special times spent together are ahead of us.

Sincere regards

David J. Gouge

TABLE OF CONTENT

ACKNOWLEDGEMENT

First off, to my family—thanks for putting up with my writing hermit mode. You guys are the real heroes, enduring my late nights and caffeine-fueled binges. Your support means the world.

To my friends—your encouragement, even when the words got stubborn, kept me going. You're not just friends; you're the characters in the story of my life, and I'm lucky to have you.

My editor deserves a special shoutout. Your patience, constructive criticism, and dedication to turning my jumbled thoughts into coherent sentences deserve all the applause.

To my readers—whether you loved it, hated it, or were somewhere in between, thanks for giving this book a chance. You're the reason I write, and I hope these words find a cosy spot in your heart.

Coffee cups, you've been my loyal companions. You've seen the messy drafts, the writer's block breakdowns, and the victorious "The End" moments. Here's to you.

Muses, you sneaky beings who drop ideas when least expected—thank you. You're the creative sparks that turned this project from a concept into a reality.

To the dreamers and wanderers—may this book be a tiny escape, a journey, or a moment of reflection in your day. I hope it brings a sprinkle of magic to your world.

To the writers who paved the way for me—your words have been my teachers, mentors, and friends. Thanks for showing me the ropes and making me fall in love with storytelling.

And, of course, to the blank pages that soaked up my ramblings, doodles, and the occasional coffee spill—thanks for being the canvas for my chaotic creativity.

This book is a team effort, a patchwork quilt of gratitude stitched together with love. Here's to the shared magic of words connecting hearts.

With all the thanks in the world,

David J. Gouge

Know about prayers yourself
10

INTRODUCTION

Understanding the Power of Prayer

Hi there, another individual searching for the extraordinary!

Have you ever gone through those quiet moments when your heart aches for goals, dreams, or the intricate fabric of life? That's when the power of prayer comes in. Rather than being just another prayer book"Know about prayer yourself"is an engaging conversation on the incredible power hidden in the heartfelt words you send out to the cosmos.

Cracking the Code on the Power of Prayer

It's a fact that praying is more than just reciting inspirational sayings or mantras. It's about launching oneself into the cosmic dialogue at the intersection of your soul and the divine. Throughout this voyage, we'll look at what makes prayer so powerful, discovering that it's more than just a ritual and that it can actually save lives by upending things in the most exquisite manner.

Your guide is "Know about prayer yourself".

Now, this is not the prayer book your grandmother used. "Know about prayer yourself" is akin to having a friend who helps you navigate the intricate web of faith, helping you to comprehend the language of prayer and showing you how to take advantage of it. We're going to talk about rules, biblical insights, and useful advice that will transform your prayer life from "meh" to "wow."

The Good News: Moving Stories

These pages are peppered with stories—not the kind of once-in-a-lifetime tales, but real, raw recollections of people who have felt the tangible miracle of prayer answered. It's similar to sharing stories with people who have gone through similar experiences over a virtual campfire. These anecdotes show that prayers are not only inspirational but also have the ability to move mountains.

Different Methods for Praying? Yes, it is true!

How do you feel? In the realm of prayer, there isn't a universal solution. It makes no difference if you decide to shout from the tops of mountains, meditate in solitude, or engage in some other activity. "Know about prayer yourself" celebrates the amazing mix of various prayer practices and helps you find the praying technique that works best for you.

Why Is It Important? Life is a journey rather than a destination because of this

Think of this book as your traveling companion through life. This trip doesn't finish with the last chapter; rather, it serves as a call to continue learning throughout your life and using the principles you've read here to tackle your daily responsibilities. We are not merely reading about prayer; we are embracing a life that is shaped by it. Are you ready to enter a level of prayer that transcends language and entails the release of a force capable of altering your life? Hurry up, let's get started!

Acknowledging the influence of prayer

Let's jump straight to the point now. Instead of only utilising words, true prayer requires a connection to something cosmic and intangible. Have you ever let those real words go out into the universe and felt a tingling sensation in your soul? That's the power we're talking about.

It's not a monologue, but a cosmic discussion.
Think of prayer as a two-way exchange of ideas. Rather than being you talking endlessly, it's a dialogue with the cosmic forces, the divine, the universe—whatever you want to call it. You will know the power of prayer when you comprehend that every word, every cry, every request is like a ping in the cosmic chatroom where your soul communicates with something far bigger than yourself.

Redefining the Rules: The Influence of Prayer

Now let's debunk the myth. It is not as simple as putting your wish list out there and hoping for a miracle. It's a revolution. It has the power to create events, rearrange the cosmic furniture, and upend your reality. Not how beautiful the words are, but rather the intention and effort you put into them, is what matters.

The Ripple Effect: How Your Prayers Affect Everything

Have you ever dropped a stone into a pond and seen the ripples grow? That stone is what your prayers are like. Rather than vanishing into thin air, they create waves that impact everything in your near proximity. You will have experienced the power of prayer when you understand that your words have the ability to travel across space and affect not only your immediate surroundings but also the greater fabric of reality.

From Heart to Universe: The Language of Prayer

No, you don't need a clandestine handshake or obscure jargon to converse with the cosmic forces. One speaks from the heart and with honesty when in prayer. It's about genuinely sharing your hopes, fears, and dreams with the universe. Understanding the power of prayer entails understanding that sincerity is the one language that speaks to everyone, everywhere, and at all times.

It's Intense and Private: Uncovering the Mysteries

This Book's Purpose: A Guide to Transformative Prayer

So, you may be asking yourself, why should I listen to "Know about prayer yourself"? A valid query. Let's dissect it.

Getting Through the Prayer Wisdom Maze

Ever felt adrift in the sea of prayer guidelines? Diverse individuals with various ideologies can be somewhat daunting. This book is meant to serve as a helpful guide for you, a compass in this wide world of prayer wisdom. We are here to help you navigate transformative prayer by cutting through the clutter and capturing the essentials.

Clarifying the Universe's Relationship

Isn't prayer typically associated with mystery? For example, what actually occurs when we pray? The aim of this book is to explain that cosmic connection in plain terms. Our goal is to simplify prayer so that it becomes something you can actually touch, experience, and relate to. The goal is to reveal the fundamental simplicity of this age-old practice, not to add more mystery to it.

Putting Theory into Practice: Using Prayer to Help You

This is a practical guide, not just a theoretical lecture on prayer. The idea is to move you from comprehending the theory to using it in real life. Our goal is to transform you into an adept in availing prayer, not to mould you into a couch potato philosopher. Sensible, doable, and designed with practical implementation in mind.

Scripture Gems and True Stories

When you can enjoy an entire buffet, why limit yourself to just one flavour? The goal is to combine poignant true stories with the timeless wisdom found in the scriptures. We're incorporating biblical tidbits and weaving them into ordinary encounters. It's about bringing the supernatural down to earth, humanising it, and demonstrating to you that this is not just some archaic folktale but also your narrative.

Increasing the Power of Your Praying Journey

This book is ultimately an empowerment tool for you. It is not intended to impose rules or a strict structure on you. Rather, the aim is to provide you with the keys to unlock the possibilities of your personal prayer experience. The idea is to give you the ability to customise your prayer practice to suit your individuality and use it as a transformational and dynamic force in your daily life.

So fasten your seatbelt. This book is meant to be your guide, advisor, and confidante as you make your way through the wide world of prayer availability. We're going on a voyage of empowerment, exploration, and transformation—we're not simply exploring. Are you prepared to jump right in? Now let's move!

Chapter 1: THE FOUNDATION OF EFFECTIVE PRAYER

Building a Strong Prayer Foundation

Think of it as laying the groundwork for a close and meaningful connection with the that will be as trustworthy as an old friend.

Regaining Fundamental Knowledge: Principles and Directives for Prayer

Do you know that a well-thought-out undertaking always starts with a plan? But creating a strong foundation for prayer is the same. Our prayer rules and standards are designed to provide you direction, not to suppress your uniqueness. Think of it as the GPS for your spiritual journey, keeping you on course even as it navigates the twists and turns of your relationship with the divine.

Every Day Observance: More Similar to a Spiritual Healing

Though they can sound a little snobbish, daily devotions are like your daily cup of coffee for the soul. It entails taking a break from your daily routine to set aside some time, throw away distractions, and tune into that cosmic frequency. It's your way of saying to the universe, "Hey, I'm here, ready to connect." Establishing a firm foundation for your prayer life begins with making this devotional activity a habit—a kind of soul-work exercise.

Seeing the Impact: Transforming Words into a Real Experience

When was the last time you saw a plant emerge from a seed? It's like the first time you start to establish a strong foundation for prayer. Your prayer takes on a life of its own and

becomes a visceral emotion. It's not just a routine; it's a dynamic dance with the otherworldly. You start to notice the ripples, the subtle shifts in perspective, the calm that settles over the chaos, and the impact.

Keeping It Simple and Real When Praying

To be honest, praying isn't about memorising a prayer or playing it out. It's about being authentically yourself. Building a strong foundation requires that you know how to pray in a style that suits you. It's about finding your rhythm, speaking from the heart, and making a real connection with the universe.

So, my friend, creating a strong foundation for prayer is like decorating a comfortable den where your spirit may rest and connect. It's a journey rather than a destination. So take your spiritual tools and let's start laying the groundwork for a very sincere relationship. Are you ready to dive straight in? Let's build together.

Establishing a Close Relationship with God

This isn't a pre-recorded performance, to start. Remember those awkward moments when you had to follow the script? Yes, but that's not the topic of this discussion. Developing a close relationship with God is less like putting on a rehearsed show and more like a freestyle rap with your heart. You without scripts, just you. That is God's awesomeness.

Heart-to-Heart Time: Being Transparent with One Another

Imagine sitting on the porch with your best friend, enjoying a cup of tea and discussing life. That is the ambiance we wish to establish. Speaking from the heart is essential to developing a closer bond with God. Elaborate sentences are not necessary; just let it flow. Talk about all the moments in between the good and the terrible. It's similar to catching up with an old friend who always finds time for you.

Speak in Your Own Tongue, and God Will Hear You

Does anyone have a friend who always finishes your sentences? That is the nature of God, but on a cosmic level. You have to develop your own connecting language in order to build a personal relationship. It's all about being real, whether that's through park walks, prayer, or meditation. God understands you even when you don't know yourself fully.

Trust your intuition; that gut feeling isn't just gas.

Do you know that gut feeling you have when something is off? Yes, that is your spiritual GPS. Trust your gut while you are developing a closer relationship with God. It's God's whisper guiding you. Pay attention to the signs and feelings that say, "Hey, I got you."

God Is Not Something You Do on Sundays: Everyday Hangs

This is not a Sunday-morning fling; this is a daily expression of affection. The first step in developing a personal relationship with God is realising that He is with you through the hectic Mondays, the chilly Wednesdays, and the "thank God it's Friday" times. It involves approaching each day as though you had a cosmic friend.

Are you ready to take this enormous guy on an emotional journey? No scripts and no formalities—just you and your cosmic confidante. Let us now go in and have an open discussion with God.

The Importance of Faith in Prayer

Faith is like the secret ingredient when it comes to praying. That's actually revolutionary because of this.

Faith: The Will to Believe Despite Not Being Able to See It

Consider faith as having faith in the Wi-Fi even when it is hidden from view. Believing that your words matter in prayer is important, even if you don't hear back right away. Faith is the lifeblood of prayer; it says, "I believe in this relationship, even before I see the fruits."

Your Spiritual Wi-Fi Passcode is Faith: Opening the Connection

Your intercessions are like an attempt to establish a WiFi connection. The secret is faith. It's what opens the door to your connection to the powerful cosmic energies. Entering the code that reads, "I believe this connection is real, and I trust that something is happening even if I can't see it," is what it means to pray with faith. Your prayers become a genuine dialogue with the cosmos when you have faith.

Increasing the Power of Your Prayers to Feed Your Spiritual Engine

Think of your prayers as a vehicle. The fuel that powers the engine is faith. Your prayers could end up trapped in the driveway without it. When you pray in faith, you are putting your words on a collision course and causing things to happen. Your words become deeds when you believe in them.

Using Faith as a GPS to Navigate Obstacles and Doubts

Doubts do indeed creep in. It is a component of the human being. However, faith? It is your compass in spirit. Faith maintains your heading even when doubts threaten to swerve you. It's the steadfast conviction that your prayers are heard and that there's a greater purpose at work, despite all the ups and downs. You can confidently travel the path of prayer with the support of your faith.

Looking Past the Visible: Religion as Spiritual Binoculars

Have you ever viewed something distant with binoculars? Faith serves as your soul's binoculars. It enables you to look past what is immediately apparent to you and beyond. When you pray with faith, you look beyond the here and now and have confidence that a larger plan is being revealed.

Providing Strength for Perseverance: As Prayer Is a Marathon, Not a Sprint

It takes a marathon to pray; it's not a sprint. And belief? It gives you more energy. When things get hard on the trip, it keeps you going. "Hang in there, keep believing," is what that inner voice says when it seems like nothing is changing. Long-term perseverance is fueled by faith.

That's the real reason why faith is the guest of honour at the prayer party. It's the crucial component that transforms your words into a potent conversation with the cosmos, not just a pleasant extra. Are you prepared to add a little faith to your prayers? Let's put it into action.

Chapter 2: PRAYING WITH CONFIDENCE

Overcoming Doubt and Insecurity

We all struggle with these feelings from time to time, but guess what? There are solutions to this situation, so you're not alone.

First of all, feeling this way is acceptable.

When uncertainty and uneasiness rap on your door, you're not broken. That's what it means to be human. Therefore, inhale deeply, name those emotions, and concede that you are not an expert.

Put your thoughts there and turn up the spotlight.

Insecurity and doubt prefer to stay in the background. Let's turn on the light. Bring those concepts to light. You can discuss them with a buddy, jot them down, or simply discuss them with yourself. Their effect on you will decrease with the amount of exposure they receive.

Examine Yourself: Who Is Your Disapproving Audience for Your Talent?

Someone's inner critic has the power to destroy a moment. Accept the challenge. "Who says I can't do this?" you ask yourself. Who declares me unworthy?" Frequently, you'll discover that it's only your inner mind talking, not a realistic fact.

Honour Your Minor Victories: You're Achieving Better Outcomes Than You Believe

Have you ever noticed how we minimise our successes? Give up the behaviour. Honour the modest victories. Completed a task? Fantastic. flawlessly delivered a presentation? Wonderful. A life is made up of all the little and big things that you accomplish. Honour and recognize them.

Recall Your Past Successes: You Have Background

Remind yourself of your prior performance if you begin to feel uncertain or uneasy. When was the last time you attempted something you weren't sure you could do well? You can overcome obstacles once more since you've done it before. Your prior accomplishments ought to be flaunted with pride, much like a superhero cape.

Speak with Someone and Split the Work

You don't have to bear the whole weight by yourself. Speak with a friend, a family member, or even an expert. You can feel less alone and learn that others have experienced similar experiences if you talk to them about your ideas and feelings.

Accept Your Flaws—They're What Make You Beautiful

It's impossible to achieve perfection. Really? Real beauty can only be found when you accept your defects. Recognize that ignorance and mistakes are normal. Life is messy, and that's just okay.

Baby steps are something you can do. Rather than Springing Into the Mountains

Leaping over mountains is not necessary to overcome doubt and anxiety. It all comes down to making little moves. Divide your objectives into more manageable, smaller activities. Any advancement—regardless of size—is a success.

You should be proud of the fact that you are a work in progress and never forget it. Though they could come knocking on your door, uncertainty and insecurity cannot take over your life. You can handle this, I'm sure.

Relying on the Promises of God

Holding fast to the beliefs that God has you covered, especially in the face of difficult circumstances and unexpected turns in life, has a great effect.

Life's Exciting Journey: Accept Its Turns and Twists

First, the obvious: you do realise that life is an emotional rollercoaster? It's acceptable to experience uncertainty, emotional highs and lows, and even stomach drops. It follows that you will sense a solid hand leading you through life if you have faith in God's promises.

The Life Manual: Citing the Promises of God

Have you ever desired a guide to life? As a result, follow the promises made by God. They have an air of assurance, as if to say, "Hey, I've got a plan, and it's a good one." Those promises, whether they be of peace, love, or a promising future, serve as a guide for this insane adventure.

Chat It Out: Discussions with the Large Man Upstairs

If doubts begin to creep in, talk to the Great Man upstairs. Consider it as a cosmic dialogue. Give God everything you have; share with Him your thoughts and worries. Relying on promises is similar to having a confidante who is always willing to listen and who knows the entire universe.

Thought: Memories of Promises Fulfilled

Has someone ever fulfilled a promise that you sincerely believed to be significant? God is not the only one who fulfils his promises, after all.Reflect on your trip, remembering the elegant times, unexpected detours, and unexpected gifts. They serve as a reminder that God keeps his promises and they are not empty words.

Being Patient and Embracing the Promise Process

Waiting isn't the most enjoyable thing, is it? However, believing God's promises frequently necessitates some waiting. It is similar to waiting for dawn after a difficult night. Although waiting is difficult, trust grows and the promise becomes even more valuable at this time.

Give It All to God: Giving Up Command

Raise your hand if you tend to be a control freak! (Holds up a hand) Leaning a little bit is often necessary when one is trusting in God's promises. It's giving up control and trusting that the universe's almighty is looking out for you. Although it's not always simple, it's freeing.

Trust Others: Together, we are in this.

This journey of trust is not yours alone. Rely on those who are also believers. Hearing about another person's experience believing in God's promises can occasionally be a lifesaver. Since we're all on this road together, some common sense goes a long way.

Honour the Unfolding: Every Aspiration Is a Step Forward

Isn't life just a sequence of moments? Every commitment kept seems like a victory. Hug them or ignore them. It's in these times that faith in God's promises becomes a living, breathing reality rather than merely an idea.

So, dear friend, remember those vows amidst life's unexpected detours. They serve as a constant reminder that a divine plan is always being carried out, much like a steadfast anchor in a storm. Have faith in that, and let the voyage proceed.

Scripture's Place in Prayer

It's very unique, I promise. It's like having a timeless discourse with the holy.

Scripture as a Forum for Discussion: The Inspired Word of God as Your Leader

Ever have a friend that always knows just what to do? Scripture is comparable to that sage buddy. It's a discourse, not a monologue. Including those verses in your prayers is like having a soul-guidebook. God's words become your cosmic conversation starter, guiding you through its many turns and turns.

Taking Solace in the Known: Similar to a Well-Worn Blanket

You know that cosy blanket you love to cuddle up in? Scripture can be used in prayer in this way. The well-known poems and emotionally stirring tales are comforting, like a warm hug. Reading scripture when things get hectic in life is like returning home to what you know; you can find comfort in words that have lasted the test of time.

Using Scripture as Your Own Songbook: Praise Songs in Old Testament Words

Have you ever found yourself humming an old song that makes you feel something? In prayer, scripture serves as your personal songbook. For example, the Psalms are like the words to the song of your soul. They communicate appreciation, anguish, and happiness. It's about taking the words that speak to you from the heart, not about being a poet.

Finding Fresh Perspectives: Lightbulb Moments in the Text

Even after reading a verse a hundred times, suddenly It strikes you in a unique way. That is the prayerful power of scripture. It's a story that is developing rather than a single

reveal. Every prayer time is an opportunity to gain fresh perspective and interpret well-known passages.

Scripture as Your GPS: Using Wisdom to Direct Your Prayers

Have you ever been lost in prayer, unsure of how to proceed with the conversation? The Bible serves as a spiritual GPS. It gives you guidance, points you in the path of wisdom, and aids in navigating the confusing terrain of prayer. It's important to have a wealth of knowledge at your disposal rather than trying to memorise every verse.

A Resource of Power: Leveraging Everlasting Resilience

Because life is unpredictable, we could all use a little extra strength. The Bible is a spiritual power bank. These are not just folktales from the past; they are tales of resilience and optimism. They give you courage by serving as a constant reminder that you are a character in a much larger story.

Scripture as a Bridge: Linking Words on Earth with Words on Heaven

Ever find it difficult to say the appropriate things in prayer? That's when the Bible acts as a link. It's similar to combining your words from this world with those from another. Scripture facilitates the real expression of one's emotions, which is all that is necessary—fancy language is not.

It is not about being a scholar, my friend, when you incorporate scripture into your prayers; rather, it is about being a seeker. It's about incorporating the ageless words into your own story and allowing them to inspire, soothe, and lead you as you go through space.

Chapter 3: THE ANATOMY OF AN EFFECTIVE PRAYER

The ACTS Model: Adoration, Confession, Thanksgiving, and Supplication

What Is the ACTS Prayer Method?

This method of praying serves as a guide or framework to assist you in organising your thoughts and desires. The acronym for prayer, thanksgiving, confession, and adoration is ACTS. This prayer model is almost a century old; it is believed to have been published in The Continent's August 1883 issue as a part of a tale series. Time spent with God is highly valued in this prayer paradigm. We come to Him in awe (adoration),acknowledge our transgressions (repentance), offer up our gratitude to Him for everything He has accomplished (thanksgiving), and finally present our requests to Him (supplication).

How Do You Modify Your Prayers Using the ACTS Prayer Method?

Sincere and heartfelt prayers are the best kind. As a result, rather than repeating exact words, you should focus on general concepts or categories. You can offer the following prayers using the ACTS prayer:

Adoration

Give thanks to God for who He is first. The second section of this prayer is thanksgiving; it is not the same as adoration since thanksgiving is an expression of gratitude to God for what He has done, whereas adoration is an expression of praise for who He is. Scripture says that God is deserving of our praise for anything He has provided or withheld from us. The only reason he is worthy is because he is God. Psalm 100:5, which reads, "For the Lord is good; His mercy is everlasting, And His truth endures to all generations," is one of the scriptures you can quote while you worship God. As an alternative, you could pray to whatever ideas the Spirit of God offers you about the majesty and merit of God's attributes and character.

Jesus commanded His disciples to start their prayers with adoration when He said, "Our Father in heaven, Hallowed [or holy] be Your name," in Matthew 6:10. You might start your prayers by giving thanks to God for all of His many blessings. For example, "Lord God in heaven, you deserve to be honoured." Since you are the origin and sustainer of life, you are God from all eternity.

Confession

The "C" in the ACTS prayer stands for confessing and acknowledging your sin to God, so that your petitions will be heard (1 Peter 3:7). Psalm 32:3-5 describes David's prayer.

"My body withered away when I remained silent about my sin."

Through my groans throughout the day.

Because of the weight of Your hand on me every day and night, my energy dissipated like the dry heat of summer. Nevermind

I came to You and admitted my sin.

"I will confess my wrongdoings to the Lord," I said, not hiding my remorse.

And You absolved the shame of my wrongdoing (NASB).

Yes, God already knows about our sins, but when we confess them, we acknowledge that God is offended by our transgressions and that we need Jesus' atonement to be freed from all sin. "But if we confess our sins to him, he is faithful and just to forgive us and to cleanse us from every wrong", according to First John 1:9.

Thanksgiving

The Bible makes it quite clear that there are other things for which we should be grateful than only what God has given us. First Thessalonians 5:18 does not state, "Give thanks in the pleasant things of life," as you might expect. Rather, it says, "Give thanks in everything; for this is God's will for you in Christ Jesus." This means that we should be grateful for everything, good or bad. As the verse states, you are doing "the will of God for you in Christ Jesus".

Give God thanks for everything, even the daily struggles you go through, the things He withholds for your good, the work He is doing in your soul to purify you, the trials that mould you into the image of Christ, and the knowledge that everything can

work together for the good of those who love Him
and are called according to His purpose (Romans
8:28).

I've found that when I begin to express thankfulness
to God for everything, not just the good things in my
life, it completely changes my perspective and
makes me feel more thankful. By giving thanks to
God for everything, we turn our attention from
ourselves and our blessings to God, the ultimate
Giver.

Supplication

This is just a formal way of saying "please." We are
told in Philippians 4:6 not to worry about anything,
but in"everything by prayer and supplication with
thanksgiving let your request be made known to
him". When we do this, we ask God for our
requests, along with a heart that is thankful for what

God has already done, as well as for what He will do.

Some Christians claim that they only pray for the blessings of others because they feel self-centred asking God for anything for themselves. However, the Bible states that if we, as naturally immoral parents, can provide our kids with excellent presents, then "how much more will your Father in heaven provide good things to those who seek Him!(Matthew 7:11).

God "withholds no good thing from those who walk with integrity," according to Psalm 84:11, and Jesus claimed in Matthew 7:7–12 that if you ask, you will get; if you seek, you will find; if you knock, you will be allowed access. Everyone who knocks will have their door opened, and those who search will find what they seek. Or who among you will give his son a stone instead of a loaf of bread when he begs for one? ..."

So feel free to knock, seek, and inquire. You might discover that God hears significantly more of your prayers than you previously believed as you proceed.

Why the ACTS Prayer Method Makes a Perfect Outline

The Acts Prayer Method can help you balance out your prayers so they are not overly self-centred, in addition to helping you stay concentrated (and prevent your mind from wandering) throughout your prayer time. Some of us approach God directly and make requests of Him without first recognizing His existence or value. While God says we can approach His throne of grace fearlessly and ask for what we need (Hebrews 4:16), how many times would you bring your wish list to a distinguished guest or a figure of power before you even acknowledged their presence, let alone the honour of being heard?

Before you ask God for whatever you need or want, the ACTS prayer makes sure you are thanking Him for everything He has done in your life, confessing sin in your heart that could otherwise prevent you from praying, and praising Him for who He is. Additionally, this prayer can provide people on the opposite end of the spectrum who are hesitant to approach God in prayer and ask for anything the assurance that there is a right time and place to do so.

Thus, why do you delay? In terms of your connection with the Most High God, there is a lot of admiring, confessing, thanking, and requesting to be done. Furthermore, He has been anticipating your spending some quality time with Him.

PRAYING CLEARLY AND WITH FOCUS

As you pray, you're trying to focus, but every now and then something else distracts you. Are you unable to recall the verses that just passed by your lips? It does take a lot of devotion to control your focus during prayer.

Prayer is seen as the link to eternity in many religions. It takes the whole presence of mind to accomplish it and receive God's gifts. Furthermore, you can only accept prayers if you pay attention.

Humans are constantly making an effort to pray sincerely. This is because everyone is aware of how crucial focus is when praying. However, there are times when it's difficult to concentrate. It's because Satan employs diversion as a means of draining your vitality and concentration.

Methods for Sharpening Your Focus in Prayer

Using reverence for God as a Focusing Technique in Prayer

Religious people think that although God created the world, it will eventually meet its end. Every human will eventually pass away and must answer to their creator. Therefore, in order to please God, we should offer our prayers with the utmost focus and sincerity.

Furthermore, keep him in mind at all times to minimise distractions. One of the things that leads to distraction is when you let love for this world overflow in your thoughts. Individuals attempt to place expectations on things that are only going to benefit them in this life. Thus, give your wishes to the Lord if you wish to protect yourself from the avarice of this world.

Even yet, you may find it difficult to let go of things at first. You can lower your expectations from this materialistic society by remembering God every day. Consequently, you will become less concerned about intrusions.

Plan Your Day While Remembering to Pray
Nothing worthwhile comes lightly;
We must put in a lot of effort to succeed. This also applies to prayerful concentrations. It's best to plan your day if you find it difficult to focus during prayers because your mind is racing with all of the things you need to get done.

Keep a journal of your daily activities and set out a specified time each day for prayer to help you focus better when you pray. A prudent individual consistently plans their movements to maximise their time. You should organise yourself and proceed with a certain goal in mind.

Timings are significant in several religions, such as Christianity. To adjust your daily schedule, you should write down the times of your prayers or use an app that provides the exact times. Making a schedule for your day will help you focus better and reduce mental strain.

Be Sure to Eliminate Anything That May Impair Your Ability to Focus During Prayer

As previously mentioned, one cause of the decline in attention during prayer is an excessive fixation on materialistic matters. To improve your ability to concentrate, you must learn to control your desires. Remembering that nothing lasts forever is one way. Furthermore, there are a variety of techniques that might assist you in eliminating distractions. First, determine what in your immediate environment is causing the greatest difficulties. After determining the sources, compile a list and devise a plan of attack.

It is not our intention to imply that you will be able to eliminate every possible distraction. It is not feasible, and you shouldn't anticipate it. The idea is that you should make an effort to reduce the things that make you less focused when you pray.

In the event that you are still unable to concentrate. The next step is to travel to a peaceful location. Rather than praying at home, you could go to the church or mosque.

One of the best methods to ignore disruptions is to alter the atmosphere. Your focus improves as a result of your sentiments being revitalised by a new environment.

Know the Bible Verses to Improve Your Focus

You will quickly become sidetracked if you are praying without knowing what you are asking for. It is among the causes of people's inability to concentrate during prayers.

The majority of prayers are said in archaic languages that are not commonly spoken. For instance, Arabic, Hebrew, Latin, etc. Therefore, in order to comprehend the book, acquire the language of the faith you practise. You will find it easier to focus if you pray to understand the significance.

God endowed his animals with the ability to reason through everything. You have no motivation to concentrate if you are unable to identify a procedure. Your interests will determine how well you concentrate. There can be no focus if there is no interest.

Furthermore, a lot of people focus all of their attention on reading the sacred passages. They become bored with it as a result since they are unable to comprehend it. You will therefore be able to discover greater curiosity if you correctly learn each verse. If you are not proficient in the language, you can also spend money on real translations.

Utilise Tidiness to Gain Focus

It's a surprisingly good idea to cleanse your body before praying. To be able to concentrate during prayer, you must be cleansed both mentally and physically.

God has made cleanliness a priority. As such, you ought to always purify yourself prior to making your requests.

Furthermore, purification might be a tactic to help focus on prayer. You feel refreshed after cleaning your body since it changes your mental condition. Thus, maintain yourself clean if you want to feel refreshed and be able to concentrate better.

A bridge that builds a connection between you and the Lord is prayer.

The only thing that can bring us and God closer is prayer. Thus, show your complete dedication if you really want to receive it. What determines whether

or not your request is fulfilled is how serious you
are.

You can use techniques like staying away from
distracting things, setting up an ideal

schedule, and when you pray, keep God in mind to
bear hardships. Consider your prayers not so much a
religious exercise as a duty, since God is always
keeping an eye on you. Your motivations should be
focused on your prayer rather than on yourself.

THE IMPACT OF GLORY IN
PRAISES

The greatest source of power that the world has not
yet seen manifested is praise. The same force that

created the earth is also the power that God has released in praise. God made people in order to be praised, according to Ephesians 1:5–6, 12. But it appears that despite all of God's wonders, humanity doesn't always give Him thanks. Rather, people frequently point the finger upon God when something goes wrong. Their own faith is hampered by this.

God is moved by faith, and thanking Him is a way we show our faith in Him. Praise unleashes His ability to act in our best interests.

When we cry out to God in disbelief, He remains unmoved. He is fully aware of our current situation and the promises He made to us. He is aware that His strength will carry us through any challenge or hardship. He will bring us through every circumstance to a point of victory if we will place our faith in Him and show that faith by giving Him praise.

We start to whine and gripe so much when things seem out of control. However, if we would give thanks to God in the midst of the circumstance, we would put ourselves in a position to receive from Him.

Let's Give God Glory!

Praise of God is our obligation. In the Book of Psalms, we witness that. Therein lies much of what the Bible says on praising. For example, the passage "Let them praise the Lord for his great love and for all his wonderful deeds to them!" appears in Psalm 107.(verse 8).

The experiences of the children of Israel are recorded in the Bible as models for us (1 Cor. 10:11). How much more should we thank our benevolent Heavenly Father if they were continually praising God in their psalms?

Men worthy of praise

Job was an Old Covenant guy who worshipped God nonstop. He gave thanks to the Lord even in the face of difficulties. Job fell before God in worship after learning that all of his children, servants, and animals had perished.

Job did not offend God even though he had boils all over his body. He went low in front of the Lord, and God delivered him. The Bible says that after Job prayed for his companions, the Lord turned his captivity and gave him double as much as he had before (Job 42:10).

David was a man of praise as well. We can get some hint of how he accomplished so in the Book of Psalms. His attitude toward God is revealed in Psalm 34.

"If we will put our faith in Him and demonstrate that faith by praising Him, He will bring us through every situation to a place of victory."

HAGIN, KENNETH W.

PSALM 34:1-3

1 I will always give thanks to the Lord and speak of him in praise.

2 My spirit will exalt her before the Lord; the lowly will hear of it and rejoice.

3 O glorify the name of the Lord with me; let us do so in unison.

David was able to give God praise. He played the harp and sang psalms. God was pleased by his praises, which repeatedly brought His anointing to the situation. For instance, King Saul would call on David to sing and play for him while he was being tormented by an evil spirit, and this would console him (1 Samuel 16:23).

Gratefulness in the Wee Hour

Paul was well-versed in giving thanks to God during difficult circumstances. He declared himself to be"crushed and completely overwhelmed,and we thought we would never live through it" (2 Cor. 1:8). And yet he gave thanks to God!

Paul did not lament the difficulties he faced in sharing the gospel. "Always rejoice in the Lord," he declared. I'll say it again: rejoice!(NKJV) Philippians 4:4.

Paul was an expert at thanking God in trying circumstances. Even at midnight, when there is no hope, Acts 16

Seemingly lost, he thanked God without waver or ceasing.

NKJV: ACTS 16:22–26

22 At that point, the throng rose up in opposition to them, and the magistrates ordered that they be beaten with rods after tearing off their clothes.

23 After giving them numerous stripes, they cast them into prison and gave the jailer orders to protect them.

24 After obtaining this accusation, he confined them to the inner jail and secured their feet in the stocks.

25 But around midnight, the convicts were listening to Paul and Silas as they prayed and sang praises to God.

26 All of a sudden, there was a powerful earthquake that rocked the prison's foundations. Everyone's chains were released and all of the doors were opened.

Since verse 23 states that they "laid many stripes on them," I assume Paul and Silas' backs were suffering from the blows they had taken. They were also presumably exhausted after spending the entire night in those stocks. However, they offered God the gift of thanksgiving. Despite their situation, they gave Him praise, even though I'm sure it wasn't what they felt like doing.

Paul and Silas remained silent and uncomplacent. They performed God's praises. What an example of faith! They did not thank God in private either, for the other inmates might hear them (v. 25).

The prison itself started to tremble as Paul and Silas sang hymns of gratitude to God. The jail trembled in the wind like a leaf!

Such a supernatural manifestation does not result by giving God "lip service" in cynical, mediocre worship. No, their emotions were expressing those accolades!

Sincere gratitude pleases God. The chains of Paul and Silas loosened and their stocks came off. All of the inmates were set free when the prison doors flew wide.

It was not because they griped and grumbled that they were completely delivered; rather, it was because they exalted God!

It's intriguing that Paul and Silas are said to have sang at midnight in the Bible. It was probably exactly midnight. However, I think that their time in prison served as a "midnight hour" in their life as well.

Many of us have the issue of exaggerating the issue rather than turning to God and magnifying Him when we find ourselves in a difficult position!

Everybody has a midnight hour from time to time. We would also feel an "earthquake" in our circumstances if we started praising God even in the face of hopelessness or impossibilities!

When all else fails, praise will bring a magnificent victory. If we will simply believe God, He will "shake" those situations that are attempting to hold us back

CHAPTER 4: PRAYING FOR PERSONAL GROWTH

PRAYING FOR WISDOM AND DISCERNMENT

Wisdom

It is important to remember that wisdom comes in two forms: wisdom from God and wisdom from the world. Who is knowledgeable and understanding among you? Allow him to prove it by his outstanding deeds and acts, which are carried out with the humility that results from wisdom. However, if your heart is filled with poisonous envy and selfish ambition, do not deny the facts or boast about it. Such "wisdom" does not come from heaven; rather, it is demonic, earthly, and unspiritual. Because envy and self-serving ambition are the root causes of disorder and all ill behaviours. The wisdom that comes down from above, however, is first and foremost pure; it is also unbiased, truthful, full of mercy and good fruit, attentive, submissive, and compassionate. By peaceful sowing, those who cultivate peace also reap righteousness.

James 3:13–18

In this verse, James employs quotation marks around the word wisdom to emphasise how, despite our own delusions to the contrary, if we are egotistical, envious or arrogant, we are merely fooling ourselves. True wisdom is obedient, kind, kind, sincere, and virtuous since God is its source.

There are more wisdom teachings in the book of Proverbs than in any other place in the Bible. True wisdom is derived from God's Word. King Solomon had the spiritual inspiration to write this book from the Holy Spirit.

"God gave Solomon great wisdom and understanding and knowledge too vast to be measured",1 Kings 4:29

The book of Proverbs has 31 chapters, so it's a great option to read one chapter every day for a month (just double up on the months with 30 days). So as I was wrapping up my 31-day study of Proverbs this morning, it occurred to me that the book speaks to every area of our lives—spiritual, physical, emotional, financial, social, and even political.

The Bible is the best source of wisdom for all of our everyday needs. I implore you to regularly read the book of Proverbs and let God's wisdom guide your thoughts.

Consider it, pray about it, jot it down, ingrain it into your mind, and think it through.

Because God is more foolish than man is intelligent, and because God is weaker than man is strong. Brothers, never forget who you were when you were called. By human standards, very few of you were wise, very few of you were of noble ancestry, and very few of you were prominent. But God chose the foolish things in the world to dishonour the wise, and God chose the weak things in the world to humiliate the powerful. (1 Corinthians 1:25-27)

Discernment

Remember that our intellect comes from the Holy Spirit. No matter how much we study and understand, we will never be able to walk in wisdom without the divine revelation of the Spirit of God.

"The Spirit of God (not the world's spirit)so we can know the wonderful things God has freely given us." This is how we communicate; we express spiritual facts using spiritual language, which is taught to us by the Spirit rather than by human intelligence. Things from the Spirit of God are incomprehensible to a man without the Spirit because they are spiritually discerned (1 Corinthians 2:12-14).

If we are not redeemed and filled with the Holy Spirit, then all of the wisdom found in the Bible is useless to us. That relationship is the key to walking intelligently and making sensible decisions that impact not only your life and family but also people around you.

The more we seek God, the more He will pour out—into our lives—His wisdom, His Word, and His Spirit.

And today, I'll pray for all of you using Ephesians 1:17 as my foundation.

"I never stop pleading with the glorious Father, God of our Lord Jesus Christ, to grant you the Spirit of wisdom and revelation so that you may know him better." Yes, in fact.

With everything that is going on in the world right now, we need judgement and wisdom. So let us seek after the things of God with diligence rather than the things of this world. Let's endeavour to learn more about Him.

Choosing to be strong in the face of weakness

We view weakness and strength as opposites. One virtue that indicates the lack of weakness is strength. The antithesis of strength is weakness. Most of us want to think of ourselves as strong. We worry that people won't think good of us if we show our frailty.

Paul appeared to be a strong guy leading a fruitful ministry. His indescribable views of paradise spurred him to strive extremely hard for the gospel and gave him the strength to endure immense adversity. "For me, living is for Christ and dying is even better" (Phil. 1:21), he was able to proclaim after seeing the glory of his destiny. But Paul never boasted about the details of his visions. He would not talk about his strength; he just revealed his powerlessness. Paul wanted people to think highly of Christ and recognize his power alone.

Accepting Our Weakness

Paul welcomed his agony. His incapacity to get rid of the "thorn" (whatever it was) or escape trying situations demonstrated the might of God at work in and through him. While Paul shared the gospel, God was working to save sinners and establish churches. God was the one with strength.

Jesus' crucifixion represented the pinnacle of power triumphing over weakness. Jesus' weakness—being mistreated, scorned, and despised—required a great deal of strength. According to Hebrews 1:3, the Son of God "upholds the universe by the word of his power." Nothing much would have needed to be done to destroy his opponents. Jesus was powerful enough to surrender to his Father and become weak for our benefit—even to the point of dying on a cross. God's wrath was appeased, the glory of the resurrection was brought, a great number of sinners were saved, and final power over sin and death was the consequence of that weakness.

Jesus uses helpless sinners to demonstrate his strength. Through our "weaknesses, insults, hardships, persecutions, and calamities," the same power that resurrected Jesus from the dead (Eph. 1:20) works inside us to make us content for the cause of Christ (2 Cor. 12:10) and to shape us to his likeness (Rom. 8:29). In order to cause us to place all of our hope in God and nothing else—the worldly things that provide us with security, comfort, and happiness—God kindly sends thorns of affliction. Jesus is our soul's lover and the one who will fulfil our most ardent desires. When we are content in our frailty, His great capacity to appease and cleanse sinners is exalted.

One day, as Christians, we will live out Paul's indescribable vision. We will celebrate when every thorn is removed and every tear is wiped away by the powerful, compassionate hand of our Saviour. For the sake of Christ, be strong today by allowing yourself to be weak. Strength and weakness are two sides of the same coin, not mutually exclusive. We are strongest when we are at our weakest (2 Cor. 12:10).

To help you find strength in your weakness, consider these three truths:

1.Our frailties serve as a reminder of God's necessity

We shouldn't be ashamed of or try to hide our flaws. We have the honour of witnessing God in our lives precisely because of our frailties.All our shortcomings serve as a constant reminder of how much we depend on God to complete us.

According to Paul in 2 Corinthians, we should all take pride in our shortcomings. We know that we have a God who can and will intervene to support us during these times.

Because of how great our God is, we can find strength in our shortcomings.

2.Recall that God's Might Is Manifested in Our Frailties

Never forget that it is in our infirmities that God's might is most effective. Instead of attempting to rely solely on our own strength, we must make space for God's power to operate inside us.

Although God's power is infinite, ours is not. We create a place for an infinite power to operate through us when we do so.

2 Corinthians 12:9 Every time, he said, "All you need is my grace." My strength is most effective

when it is weak. I am happy to now brag about my shortcomings in order to allow Christ's power to operate through me.

We must see our frailties and faults as opportunities for God to strengthen us. They are intended to let God manage things rather than to embarrass or demoralise us.

Corinthians 12:10 For this reason, I enjoy my shortcomings as well as the taunts, tribulations, persecutions, and problems I go through in the name of Christ. Because I am strongest when I am weak.

3.God Does Great Things Using Our Weaknesses

Recall that God does tremendous things through using our shortcomings. The Bible contains numerous passages that demonstrate how God can use human frailties for the benefit of the kingdom.

Despite Moses' speech impairment, God called Moses to address the pharaoh in the book of Exodus.

In 1 Samuel 16, despite being the youngest, God appointed David as king. The list is endless.

God can make use of our frailties.

Exodus 4:10–12 However, Moses begged the LORD, saying, "Lord, I'm not very good with words." Despite the fact that you have spoken to me, I am not and have never been. My words become jumbled and I become tongue-tied. The LORD then questioned Moses, saying, "Who makes a person's mouth? Who makes the decisions about whether or not people hear, see, or speak? I, the LORD, am I not? Proceed now! I'll be by your side while you talk, giving you advice on what to say.

Use this as a chance to rely on God the next time you're feeling down, having trouble with something, feeling inadequate, etc.

Allow your difficulties to serve as a reminder that even in your weakness, God is strong enough to stand by you.

CHAPTER 5: PRAYING FOR OTHERS

Intercessory Prayer: Standing in the Gap

What is intercessory prayer?

Prayer for the needs of others is known as intercessory prayer. Offering up prayers for others is a selfless way to show love.

God commands us to pray for others, but why? Because God's own kind, loving nature is reflected in intercessory prayer. God wants us to think as He does, and we can think beyond ourselves and develop compassion for others by praying for them. Prayer is like fragrant incense that God finds pleasing (Revelation 5:8).

For whom shall we offer prayers?

Throughout the Bible, God instructs us to pray for others in multiple instances. James, the apostle, instructs us in James 5:16 to "pray for one another, that you may be healed."

The apostle Paul exhorts us to pray for ministers and members of the church.

"Being watchful to this end with all perseverance and supplication for all the saints—and for me, that utterance may be given to me, so I may open my mouth boldly to make known the mystery of the gospel, for which I am an ambassador in chains—and praying always with all prayer and supplication in the Spirit".

In order for us to live a tranquil and peaceful life in complete godliness and reverence, Paul exhorts us "that supplications, prayers, intercessions, and giving of thanks be made for all men, for kings and all who are in authority" (1 Timothy 2:1-2).

Therefore, we are even expected to pray for public officials and other people who may not be aware of our existence and who have not requested our prayers.

According to Matthew 5:44, Jesus Christ even gave the following command: "Love your enemies, bless those who curse you, do good to those who hate you, and pray for those who spitefully use and persecute you."

The model of intercessory prayer set by Jesus

While going through His most difficult ordeal, Jesus prayed a lot. If you had been faced with death or torture, what would you have prayed for? It's interesting to observe what Jesus was thinking about when He prayed, not just for Himself (Luke 22:41–42), but also for His followers and for everyone of us:

"Just as You sent Me into the world, so I have sent them into it. And I purify Myself for their sakes, so that the truth may sanctify them as well.

In addition to those who will accept Me via their word, I pray for those who will be one in Us so that the world will acknowledge that You sent Me. This is what John 17:18–21 says about praying for them. Jesus did not limit His attention to Himself; rather, He made it clear to His followers that He desired all the blessings of the Holy Spirit, including love, joy, peace, and patience (John 13–17).

He prayed for them—and us—out of love and genuine concern, knowing that His trial would be their trial and that "the sheep will be scattered" (Mark 14:27) when He, the good Shepherd, was hit.

According to Romans 8:34 and Hebrews 7:25, Jesus Christ is our Intercessor because He experienced the ups and downs of a human life and can relate to our weaknesses. He also makes it possible for us to approach the "throne of grace" and receive the mercy and assistance we require.

(Read Hebrews 4:15–16). He also desires that we develop our intercessory skills.

False beliefs on intercessory prayer

Prayer intercession is not a maths exercise. God can step in to help a situation without waiting for ten, twenty, or even hundred people to pray about it. Prayer is neither a ballot or a request that God must grant just because enough people "sign" it. God cannot act in response to our requests.

When the moment is right, God can and will intervene, whether a single person or a million people pray for it. See our article "God's Timing Is Perfect" for more information about God's timing.

Furthermore, we shouldn't use intercessory prayer as a way to gain favour with God.

in case something unfortunate were to happen to us. Our driving force needs to be love—selfless, extroverted care.

And what about the one requesting prayer? Is it possible for someone to ask believers to pray for them and then feel that they don't need to pray for themselves?

No, praying cannot be delegated. Whether or not other people are praying for us, we still need to go to God in earnest since prayer is an integral aspect of our relationship with Him personally.

How to offer prayers on behalf of others

Our relationship with our benevolent heavenly Father is mostly mediated via prayer. He explains in the Bible how to pray in a way that pleases Him, which is the most effective method to pray.

These are some scriptural guidelines for successful intercessory prayer. We ought to:

Express your sincere and profound feelings for other people in your prayers.

Offer up prayers for other people on a regular basis. Jesus instructed us to pray, "Give us this day our daily bread," in what is commonly referred to as the Lord's Prayer (Matthew 6:11; see "The Lord's Prayer"). Every day, we ought to pray for both our needs and other people's needs.

Pray in depth for other people. God is all-knowing, but He invites us to bring all of our unique needs to Him because He enjoys communication and wants to know what's important to us. According to Leviticus 16:12, God appreciates prayers that are like "sweet incense beaten fine." The Bible compares our prayers to incense. Praying in detail and with thoughtfulness is more pleasing than saying a quick prayer to "bless everybody." You can recall the specifics by keeping a prayer list or prayer journal.

Pray for others with faith, understanding that God is all-powerful and that those for whom we pray are loved. Faith serves as a reminder that God is aware of what is ultimately best for every individual and that, despite His sometimes unsatisfactory answers, we may always have faith that He is acting in our best interests.

Offer loving prayers for others. Keep in mind that the names on a prayer list are actual individuals with genuine needs, hardships, and emotions. Remember that God loves all of them and desires that we show the same unwavering compassion for them. The core of God's nature is unselfish love, or godly love.

Offer up prayers for other people with zeal, fervour, and intensity. "The effective, fervent prayer of a righteous man avails much," according to James 5:16.

Offer up prayers for those who are in need of our assistance. This could involve encouraging words and hands-on assistance. Visits, calls, and cards could be beneficial. If telling someone you are praying for them will help them feel encouraged, then it is OK.

Every now and then, fast and pray for others. You may choose to fast and pray to get closer to God and offer your request to Him when something is really serious or affects you personally.

Scripture texts urging us to pray for others

Studying and reflecting on the numerous instances of people praying for others found in the Bible can teach us a great deal. A few instances of intercessors found in the Bible are as follows:

For the benefit of his nephew Lot, Abraham pleaded on behalf of the Sodomites (Genesis 18:23–33). His famous first question was whether God would save

Sodom if there were fifty righteous individuals present. He next requested, in a bold yet humble manner, about forty, thirty, twenty, and ultimately ten. God said, "I will not destroy it for the sake of ten," even though He was unable to find ten. Nevertheless, by sparing Lot and his family, God accomplished Abraham's intention.

God's mercy for the sinful people of Israel was beseeched by Moses (Exodus 32:9–14; Numbers 14:11–20). Moses declined God's invitation to create a country from the descendants of Moses, and they fervently pleaded for God's pity in the cause of God.

Daniel (Daniel 9:3–19) pleaded with God for his people. Daniel concludes his heartfelt and contemplative prayer with the words, "O Lord, hear! Please pardon, O Lord! Lord, hearken and respond! God, you have called Your city and people by Your name; therefore, do not delay for Your own sake (verse 19).

Acts 9:36–41 says that as the apostle Peter prayed for the cherished Dorcas, God even brought her back to life.

Apostolic prayer for the people he served was a regular practice for the apostle Paul (Romans 1:9–10; 10:1; Ephesians 1:15–19; Philippians 1:3–11; 1 Thessalonians 3:9–13).

PRAYING FOR DEAR ONES

One of the greatest things you can do for your loved ones is to pray for them. God has commanded us to pray for those in our immediate vicinity as well as for ourselves, especially our friends and family. "Love each other with genuine affection," says Romans 12:10. surpass each other in displaying honour.

Prayer is never in vain, that much is certain of it. Thanksgiving with loved ones is therefore always beneficial. When we most need a response, God will grant all of our prayer requests.

Our daily prayer time should include a prayer for our friends and family. Every time we offer up a prayer for ourselves, let's not forget our friends and family.

Saying a prayer for friends and family

I ask the Lord, my God, to watch after and lead all of my loved ones on a daily basis. Lord, satisfy all of their needs and grant them everything of their heart's desires. Take care of them and make sure they have good health for the rest of their life.

God and my Lord, keep my friends and family safe. Keep them well away from tyranny. I won't hear negative things about any of them from anyone. They will all survive to see the results of their labour and won't pass away prematurely.

O Lord, reach out to the hearts of those who have not yet accepted you (you might call them names).

into their existence. In order for them to acknowledge you as the dependable Saviour, touch their hearts. In the powerful name of Jesus, touch them so they might experience the joy of salvation. Indeed.

A Prayer of Thanksgiving for Our Loved Ones

I give thanks to you, O Lord, my God, for surrounding me with kind people. We appreciate you being their source of happiness and supporting them through their struggles. Thank you, Lord, for sustaining and fortifying them. I give you thanks for bestowing onto them all of life's wonderful treasures. In Jesus' name. Indeed.

Praying for the Safety of Your Family

Some families are geographically separated. Even though it can be difficult, their faith in the Lord is strengthened because they put their trust in Him that everything will work out. Never forget that God is always watching out for our families.

Dear God, I am grateful that You always keep my family secure and safe. Even if we might not be together at the moment, I have faith that we are still a strong, cohesive family in our hearts. Regardless of how close or distant we may be from one another, our shared faith unites us. I hope and pray that my family members stay safe. I am aware that no matter where we are in the globe, You are constantly keeping watch over us and protecting us. We are grateful to the Lord for keeping us safe. We are always safe when we put our trust in You, therefore may we as a family never lose sight of Your direction. In the name of Christ, our Lord, I pray this. Amen.

Saying a Blessings Prayer

All benefits originate from You, Father God of benefits. I ask that You bless and keep my loved one above and beyond my own requirements. Assist them and bestow Your favour upon them. Grin at them and bestow onto them Your serenity. Fill their days with awe at Your kindness toward them and place Your Holy Spirit within them. Make them happy as they partake in Your holy people's inheritance in Your light-filled kingdom. Indeed.

Offerings in Prayer for Eternal Guardianship

The evil one prowls around like a lion looking to eat someone, but according to Your Word, O Jehovah, mighty Father, everyone who rebels against us will be humiliated and ashamed. You claim that everyone who opposes us will vanish and become nothing. Father, get my loved one ready for everyday spiritual combat. Cover them with God's whole Armour. Keep them safe from the devil's scorching arrows. May You chastise the evil one and may Your angels keep watch. I am aware that we are victorious because of Christ. Indeed.

Praying to Help You Make the Best Choices

You guide the paths of those who love You, Holy God of light. I ask that You lead my loved one in all of their decisions through Your Spirit. I am aware that they will soon need to make some important choices. I acknowledge that I am unsure about the best path. However, You do. You claim that anybody who asks receives Your wisdom without charge. Now, I beseech You to provide them the discernment to recognize what is best for them to do. Give wisdom and profound insight, and a breadth of understanding as limitless as the sand on the seashore, as You did for Solomon, God. I ask in the name of Jesus. Indeed.

Asking for Wisdom in Prayer

Give this person I adore insight, precious Holy Spirit. Fill them with Your spiritual wisdom and understanding for both the major and small decisions of daily living. Give them the wisdom from heaven, which is pure, loving peace, thoughtful, and merciful. Make them a mediator if they encounter difficult circumstances. Lead their steps throughout the hard times so that they may most glorify You. I adore, praise, and offer credit to You because of Your wisdom, which is more valuable than any ruby or earthly wealth! Indeed.

Praying to Recognize Sin

Freedom exists in the grace of the Almighty God, the Creator and Sustainer. It is not, however, an excuse to sin. Make my loved one see that sin ultimately results in suffering and ruin. Lead them to the liberty provided by Your directives. God, You have called each of us by name, and You will pardon those who turn to You and turn from their evil deeds. Give my loved one a burning desire to turn from their sins and pursue God's kingdom and Your righteousness. Use me to demonstrate Your goodness to my loved one. I pray in the kind and kind name of my Lord and Savior, Jesus Christ. Indeed.

A Repentance Prayer

I come to You, Heavenly Father, with a heavy heart. I adore this person, and even though I'm sure they understand right from wrong, they still lead a sinful life. Change their hearts to allow them to put on Your new, authentic selves. Tell them they are Yours and that they were purchased at a cost. Tell them that their days are limited and that life is a transient state. Let them enter the doorway You have opened to eternal life with You, and open their spiritual ears to hear Your truth. We are grateful that You sent Your Spirit to guide us along Your paths. Indeed.

supplication for peace

My loving God, I ask that You calm my loved one's thoughts and instil Your serenity in their heart. Your calm, which above comprehension, fills them. Lord, keep them and bless them. May You bless them and have mercy on them for the rest of their lives. Take out the anxiety-inducing spirit in them. Jesus came into the world to give us life—life abundantly. I hope and pray that they will come to realise this truth. May they experience the fruit of joy in their lives as they walk by Your Holy Spirit. I ask in the name of Your dear Son, Jesus Christ. Indeed.

For the family, why do we pray?

Every person's first life experiences are primarily formed within their family. Our families are the first environments in which we are predominantly shown love and taught valuable life lessons. People who grow up in dysfunctional families typically don't make good people. It is necessary for family members to pray in order to experience the serenity that fortifies the bonds within our family.

What makes us pray for our friends and family members?

Man is not an island. Everybody needs a support system from time to time. Our buddies are just as important as our family. There are still a lot of people in the world who make better friends, even though a lot of others have gotten themselves involved with toxic friendships. Proverbs 17:17 in the Bible states, "A brother is born for adversity, and a friend loves at all times."

The Value of Prayer for Friends, Family, and Loved Ones

Praying for those around us is the most beneficial thing we can do for them. The Bible commands us to do this, so we must. Giving gifts is just one way to demonstrate your brotherly love; you can also express your affection by praying for and with friends and family. Never fail to offer prayers of gratitude to loved ones for everything that God has done for them.

PRAYING FOR RECOVERY AND HEALING

How to Pray for Restorative & Healing

Does God still heal people today? He does, of course! God heals financial, physical, mental, emotional, relational, and other types of pain in diverse ways. Whether we realise it or not, we all require some form of repair or healing since we live in a broken world. I would outline four requirements on this page that must be met for any aspect of our lives to be healed and restored. Find out why seeking God, being humble, praying, and depending on his Word can lead to forgiveness and healing.

"I will hear from heaven, and I will forgive their sins, and I will heal their land IF my people who are called by my name will humble themselves and pray, and seek my face, and turn from their wicked ways" (Chronicles 7:14 NLT)

Four circumstances

I'm not in control, admit it!

2 Chronicles 7:14a "If my people will humble themselves..."

HUMILIA:

I will be guided by God if I am humble.

Psalm 25:9 (TEV) states, "God leads the humble in the right way and teaches them his will."

I'll be blessed by God if I'm humble.

Isaiah 66:2 (NLT) states, "I will bless those who have humble and contrite hearts."

God will give me the ability to change if I am humble.

James 4:6 says, "God opposes the proud but gives grace to the humble."

God will relieve my stress if I am humble.

In Matthew 11:29, Jesus says, "Take up my yoke and learn from me; for I am gentle and humble, and I will restore deep rest to your soul."

Action Plan: Use the verses for each area during your prayer time and present these areas to God. This week, concentrate on one of these areas each day.

APPLY FOR HELP FROM GOD!

"Should my people... pray..." 2 Chronicles 7:14b

As you haven't asked for anything in my name up to this point, Jesus says, "I tell you the truth: my Father will give you anything you ask for in my name. Ask and you'll receive, so that your joy will be the fullest possible joy" (John 16:23–24);

NEVER FORGET WHAT JESUS WANT ME TO ASK

USE JESUS' NAME TO ASK

"And the prayer offered in faith will make the sick person well; the Lord will raise him up. If he has sinned, he will be forgiven. Is any one of you in trouble? He should pray. Is anyone happy? Let him sing songs of praise. Is anyone sick? He should call the elders of the church to pray over him and anoint him with oil in the name of the Lord." James 5:13–15 (NIV)

"Always be ready and never give up! ALWAYS pray for ALL God's people! Pray in the Spirit at ALL times with ALL kinds of prayers, asking for ALL you need," according to Ephesians 6:18 (NCV).

Action plan: Make a list of the above five actions, post them anywhere you often spend quiet time, and remind yourself of them every day.

Go after God, not miracles!

Assuming that my people will seek my face, 2 Chronicles 7:14c

Proverbs 8:17 states, "I love those who love me, and those who seek me find me."

Hebrews 11:6b (NIV) states, "God rewards those who earnestly seek him."

"You will return to the Lord your God and obey him when you are in distress and all these things have happened to you. For He is a merciful God; he will not abandon or destroy you. If you seek the Lord your God, you will find him IF you look for him with all your heart and with all your soul." Deut. 4:29–31a (NIV)

"Prize first his kingdom and his righteousness, and you will receive all these other things as well," says Matthew 6:33.

CHANGE MY VIEW OF THE WORLD TO THE WORD

2 Chronicles 7:14d "If my people turn from their wicked ways..."

Proverbs 28:13 (NCV) states, "You will not succeed if you conceal your sins; but, if you confess and reject them, you will receive mercy."

James 5:16 (NIV) says, "Therefore confess your sins to each other and pray for each other so that you may be healed."

Know about prayers yourself
114

Chapter 6: Prayers for Specific Needs

PRAYING FOR FINANCIAL BLESSINGS

How to pray for financial blessings?

We can find solace and direction in praying for financial blessings as we work to manage your resources and attain financial security. The power of prayer may help us discover the courage and clarity we need to make the correct decisions, whether we are dealing with financial difficulties, trying to save money for retirement, or just trying to be good stewards of what we have. We petition God for wisdom in managing our finances, the bravery to take calculated risks when needed, and blessings of wealth and abundance in these prayers for financial blessings. May these prayers help you discover the stability and security you desire while holding fast to your religious beliefs, and may they also help you get closer to your financial objectives.

Gratitude for Monetary Benefits

Please, God I am grateful for all of the benefits you have bestowed upon me. I beg for your ongoing support and direction as I handle my money. Grant me the discernment to make prudent financial choices and assist me in being a good steward of the assets you have entrusted to me. I ask that you bless my money and meet my necessities so that I can support the work of your kingdom and contribute freely to others.

Lord With sad heart, I came to you today, trying to support my family and make ends meet. In this hour of need, I pray for your financial abundance and ask for your assistance. Assist me in putting my confidence and trust in your provision, knowing that you will supply all of my needs in accordance with your glory and riches. I ask that you give me additional opportunities to earn more money and support my family, and that you give me judgement and wisdom in handling my finances.

Dear God Almighty, I am incredibly grateful for all of your blessings, especially the money I have been able to save. I ask that you keep providing my family and I with security and plenty in our finances so that we can support the work of your kingdom and contribute freely to others. Assist me in making prudent and accountable financial choices, and in allocating my resources to serve others and you in gratitude. Give us the fortitude and bravery to put our faith in your provision, and please supply all of our needs in accordance with your riches in glory. Indeed.

Heavenly Father, I come to you now to beg for a financial boon so that I can better my life.

My faith sustains me, and I have confidence that you will take care of my loved ones and myself.

I'm not looking for big bucks.

I don't bother you with unnecessary luxuries or conveniences.

I just want enough money to get by financially and to reduce my stress.

Give me the tools I need to carry out your tasks and share your love.

If given the opportunity, I would be able to contribute so much more.

I ask in your name. Thank you.

PRAYERS FOR HEALTH AND HEALING

God's Word is life to us and health to all our flesh (Proverbs 4:22), so God's words are what have been incorporated into the prayer below, along with His thoughts regarding your healing and well-being. Saying this prayer aloud often as you make it your confession can help you create a positive mental picture of health in your heart. You will awaken faith in your heart and become more firmly anchored in the reality that you are a new creation in Christ Jesus (Romans 10:17).

Recall that God fulfilled His Word by keeping an eye on it (Jeremiah 1:12). He follows the instructions in His Word, and it does not come back to Him empty (Isaiah 55:11). You will therefore experience healing in your life once your words—supported by faith—align with God's words!

Papa, I confidently approach Your throne in hopes of receiving grace to assist when I'm in need. I put my trust in Your Word, and I cling to Your promises of healing. Isaiah 53:5 and 1 Peter 2:24 both state that I ward from illness and disease. I believe in my heart that I am healed of all illness and disease, and I speak with my mouth.

According to what Your Word says, Jesus carried my sorrows and all of my illnesses, thus I am now healed. I affirm that Jesus is my Healer. I know this. I am very grateful to You for providing me with what I require to live in wholeness.

I am grateful for my long life, which fulfils me. Thank You, Father, that You show no regard for human dignity. You will extend Your kindness to everyone who asks and has confidence in You.

In the name of Jesus, I announce that you are powerless over me, Satan. Matthew 18:18 states, "I bind you from acting in any way against me." In Christ, my life is concealed. You are utterly helpless to impart any portion of the curse upon me. As one who has been freed from the curse, I declare my intentions. You have to run for it now! I reject you and accept my place in God.

Father, I adore You now. You have my respect. I humbly acknowledge that Your Word will not come back to You empty. I thank You for keeping me safe and for Your kindness in my life. I'm grateful that Satan can't get through it. I am grateful that You have completely healed me. According to Your Word, I shall receive anything I ask for in the name of Jesus. So I'm going to call this done. I've fully recovered. Indeed.

WANTING PEACE AND COMFORT

The God of peace and all comfort is our Heavenly Father. God is the only one who can bring comfort and serenity during difficult times. The Bible gives us solace during difficult times, regardless of our strength and bravery or lack thereof. God is our strength and haven. Keep your hearts from being disturbed.

The promise of God's peace is seen throughout the Bible. In order to rescue us from our sins and bring us peace from evil, Jesus Christ gave His life. We have put together a compilation of comforting Bible verses regarding God's peace and comfort in case you feel like you are living in the valley of the shadow of death right now. We pray that these reassuring Bible passages will provide you serenity and tranquillity throughout the storm.

Bible verses that offer consolation and tranquillity

31:8–9 Deuteronomy The Lord himself will accompany you and go before you; he will never desert you. Do not let fear or discouragement overcome you.

14:27 in John I give you my serenity, and I leave you with yours. I do not provide you what the outside world offers. Keep your hearts calm and don't allow fear to control you.

23:4 Psalm I won't dread evil, even though I'm walking down the deepest valley, since you're with me. Your staff and rod give me comfort.

Psalm 27:1 Whom should I fear? The Lord is my light and my salvation."The fortress of my life is God"; who should I fear?

Psalm 27:12 Whom should I fear? The LORD is my light and my rescue. My life is a stronghold in the Lord; who should I fear?

Isaiah 41:10 Have no fear, because I am your God. I will strengthen you, assist you, and sustain you with my righteous hand. Do not be alarmed.

Isaiah 43:1–2. You need not be afraid, for I have called you by name, redeemed you, and claimed you as mine. I will accompany you when you cross the seas, and the rivers won't sweep you away when you cross them. You will either burn or be consumed by the flames as you move through the inferno."

Chapter 7: The Role of Persistence in Prayer

Our prayers won't always be heard. Why should we keep praying if there's no assurance that our prayers will be heard?

Jesus directly addressed this matter in Luke 18:1–8:

THE PARABLE OF THE PERSISTENT WIDOW

And he related a tale to them, encouraging them to never give up and to never lose hope. "There was a judge in a certain city who neither feared or respected God," he stated. And he was frequently approached by a widow in that city who begged him to "give me justice against my adversary." He refused for a long, but eventually said to himself, "Even though I don't fear or respect God, I will give this widow justice so that she won't keep coming back and beating me down." "Hear what the unrighteous judge says," declared the Lord. And when his elect cry out to him day and night, will God not grant them justice? Will he put them off for too long? He will swiftly serve them with justice, I assure you. Will the Son of Man, however, find faith on earth when he arrives?

Three reasons are given in Luke 18:1–8 to continue praying:

1. The Delightfulness of God (v. 7)

2. The Magnificence of God (v. 8a).

3. The Glory of God (verse 8b)

First of all, since the God we serve is genuinely kind, we ought to continue being firm in our prayer lives. I can still clearly recall the day this idea came to me: My wife and kids returned to our street after a lengthy stroll. Our son was so excited and enthusiastic as they got closer to our house that he ran inside to do his very favourite activity, which is to ring the doorbell. My spouse was aware of his actions, but she was also aware that I wasn't at home. She reduced her speed and observed. She was surprised that even in the absence of a response, he continued. Rather, he rang the doorbell with more determination. The Lord softly spoke to me as my wife told me this tale again, saying, "This is how you should pursue me in prayer." However, why did my son keep ringing the doorbell when he didn't get a response? It's easy: he thought I was a nice father. If he kept ringing, he thought, 1) he would finally catch my attention and, 2) if I was home, I would accept him with joy. He wouldn't be left behind a locked door by myself. He wouldn't ring the bell if he didn't think those things were true. Persistent prayer is analogous to making a commitment to acknowledge and respond to God's goodness.

The question "And will not God..." in our text best illustrates the goodness of God. (v7). Take note of the two fallacies we oppose: God is unjust. Furthermore, God is unconcerned. Is the "god" you worship good? Pray and keep ringing the doorbell of God's goodness. It's right that you persisted with him.

Second, because the God we serve is so great, we should continue to be firm in our prayer lives. Jesus calls Himself "The Son of Man," which is His favourite moniker, in verse 8. Jesus is the one sovereign who possesses absolute power, beyond that of any king, judge, or ruler (Daniel 7:14). Now for the reasoning: How much more would the mighty and sovereign creator grant his children's prayers if an earthly judge, who neither reveres nor fears God, can alter his decision due to a widow's tenacity? Beseeching God for a blessing is not the goal of persistent prayer; rather, persistent prayer is the understanding that God is the blessing, capable of providing what He wants, at His own pace.

Third, we ought to continue to be unwavering in our prayer lives because the God we serve is deserving of all praise. Jesus responds to the query, "Why should we pray and not give up," in verse 8. Faith, to put it simply. "Will the Son of Man find faith on Earth when he comes?" he asks. The expression of what we take to be true is called faith. Moreover, it is hard to please God without faith because anyone with access to supernatural energy and strength is a great comfort: According to Isaiah 40:31, "But those who wait on the LORD shall renew their strength; they shall mount up with wings like eagles, they shall run and not grow weary, they shall walk and not faint." "Wait on the LORD; be of good courage, and He shall strengthen your heart; wait, I say, on the LORD," echoes the psalmist. (Psalm 27:14).

Another prerequisite for understanding God's timing is trust. Actually, our ability to wait on the Lord is greatly influenced by how much we trust in Him. When we completely rely on God and refuse to rely on our own, often inaccurate assessment of the circumstances, He will lead us (Proverbs 3:5–6). "The man who trusts in the LORD is surrounded by His unfailing love" (Psalm 32:10, emphasis added). But we have to get to know God before we can really trust him. Furthermore, the best way to learn about Him is through His Word. God imparts His divine vigour into our lives through His inspired Word (1 Thessalonians 2:13). Scripture accomplishes the following: it fortifies (Psalm 119:28), directs (Psalm 119:105), guards (Psalm 119:114,117), instructs and trains (2 Timothy 3:16–17), enlightens us (Psalm 119:97–100), and saves (Romans 10:17; 1 Peter 1:23). If we routinely study and consider His Word, we will likewise be able to detect His timetable.

Usually, when we question God's timing, it's because we're looking for guidance or comfort from a difficult situation. However, we can have faith that our heavenly Father always knows exactly where we are in life. For His perfect reason, He either put us there or is allowing us to remain there. In reality, God often uses hardship to strengthen our patience, allowing our Christian faith to develop and mature to its fullest (James 1:3–4). Moreover, we know that all things work for the good of those who love God in the end, even these difficult times (Romans 8:28). God does hear His children's cries, and He will answer in a way that best fits His plan and timing. "A righteous man may have many troubles, but the LORD delivers him from them all," states Psalm 34:19. Jeremiah 29:11 tells us that God loves His children and wants the best for them, not the worst for them.

Know about prayers yourself
134

Chapter 8: Developing a Consistent Prayer Life

CREATING A PRAYER ROUTINE

Here are five suggestions for developing a consistent prayer practice if you've been looking for a means to improve your prayer life.

1. Be Practical With Your Daily Prayer Schedule

Set goals, even lofty ones. Setting impractical expectations, or pushing the envelope too far too quickly, can, in the end, result in disappointment and complete idea abandonment. Thus, if you approach your new prayer practice realistically, you'll really stick with it!

Don't try to get up at five in the morning if you wake up at eight every morning. At least not straight away. Choose a difficult but long-term achievable task. Don't aim for an hour if you're already stressed for time in the morning. Set modest initial targets, such as 10 minutes, and gradually increase them until you reach your desired end point.

You will have a better chance of forming a lifelong habit of prayer if you approach it gradually.

Watch Victory to receive more insightful prayer advice!

2. Establish the Goal of Your New Prayer Practice

If, when it comes time to pray, you have no intention of praying for anything specific, you can end up feeling as though your time has been wasted. You will not follow through on this idea!

While you should undoubtedly follow the Holy Spirit's guidance, it's advisable to make a plan of action beforehand. Your goal might seem something like this, for instance:

• Offer prayers of praise and worship to the Lord on behalf of your country, city, church, pastors, and anybody else that comes to mind.

• Express your needs to God for your family and yourself.

You won't have trouble starting if you know that worshipping and praising the Lord will be your initial action. You'll immediately enter a state of worship and optimise your time.

3. Select a Location for Your New Daily Prayer Practice

Where is a good place to pray? Do you enjoy spending time outside on a patio or deck? Which room in your house is the quietest? Pick a spot where you can be alone and quiet without being bothered by kids, spouses, or dogs. You're more inclined to persevere in the long term if you know you'll have this time to yourself.

Make sure your Bible, Scripture book(s), and Communion items are easily accessible. Arrange a cosy chair in your space if you prefer to sit while you pray.

4. Establish a Time Limit for Your New Prayer Practice

Start with 10 or 15 minutes a day and work your way up to an hour if that's your goal. Put a timer on for the length of time you want to spend in prayer so you won't be distracted by the time all the time.

Once a week or two has passed, increase your time by 10 minutes at a time until you have reached your target. However, don't adhere too closely to a set period of time. In ten minutes of focused, intense, faith-filled prayer, you can move heaven and earth, but in sixty minutes of rambling, you won't get anything done!

You'll be more likely to stick with your objective if you manage your time well and know you have a plan for the remainder of the day.

5. Continue with Your New Prayer Schedule

Don't give up on your new prayer practice if you can't seem to get up early enough each day or if you can't seem to find the time you need to pray! There will be days when you simply cannot get up and days when you have nothing to pray for. It's okay!

Establishing a goal should not make you become legalistic, but rather provide you with something to strive for. Simply pick it up the following day if you miss it the first. The Lord will meet you in your prayer time and make Himself known to you if you are spending quality time with Him. After that, you won't feel like it's a chore since you'll want it so much.

You will persevere if you establish a new prayer routine using these five suggestions! More significantly, it will alter your day's course when you start prioritising your needs. A great way to prepare your heart for the day and start the process of breakthroughs is through prayer. Thus, begin to pray

Overcoming Typical Prayer Obstacles

We encounter two main difficulties and barriers in our prayer journey.If we want our prayers to be effective, we must address these issues.

These are the issues and solutions to them.

TIMES

Regardless of the state of our lives, we are busy. And we frequently neglect to pray because of our hectic schedules.
Please allow me to share these recommendations to help you overcome if time is your challenge.

Methods for Triumphing

Give prayer first importance. Make a note of prayer and set a reminder. Yes, I am aware. When you initially hear this advice, you might feel a little uncomfortable because it seems a little sacrilegious. Please be patient with me. Have you not discovered that planning ahead is the most effective strategy to ensure that family or romantic night occurs? Consider scheduling a reminder alert on your phone or noting your prayer times on your calendar.

Analyse your life. Take a few days to observe where and how you are spending your waking hours. Next, search for locations where you can

As you live, pray. Our heavenly father is reachable from anyplace at any time. When you get your coffee in the morning, do the laundry, walk the dog, or wait in line at the groceries, think about saying a prayer.

Find a prayer style that suits your wiring. It's a proven fact that we prioritise the things we love. Do you like to spend time outside admiring God's creation? Then say a prayer while strolling across the park. Do you think deeply? Seek out a peaceful area to engage in reflective prayer.

TEXT

Not knowing "what" to pray for is the other major challenge that a lot of us deal with. Maybe there are too many things on our minds, or there are too many things to divert us. I admit that there are days when it's just hard for me to think. For whatever reason, we find ourselves praying incoherently and broadly on behalf of the people we are praying for.

Ways to Overcome
Pray Particularly: The Bible makes reference to praying specifically. As any human would, Elijah offered a very particular prayer. Be alert; scan and listen for needs before offering up a prayer.

"Elijah was a guy like us in nature. He prayed a lot that it would not rain, and the earth was spared rain for three years and six months. Once more, he prayed, and this time, heaven sent rain and the soil produced fruit.

James 5:17–18

Ask: So easy, but so frequently forgotten. Asking will help you get requests for prayers. It just takes a few seconds. Text someone. Give someone a call.

One of the finest strategies to get past the difficulty of knowing what to pray is to pray the scripture. There's no wrong way to pray the Scriptures. It is both particular and biblical. Of course, you can pray any passage of Scripture, but if you are new to this practice, you might choose to start with one of Paul's or the Psalms' prayers.

It will require work, intention, and commitment to overcome the obstacles. Put another way, labour, but worthwhile labour.

Additionally, labour involves more than just overcoming obstacles. Prayer is WORK, as Oswald Chambers once stated.

A QUIET PLACE IS IMPORTANT

Every Christian knows how crucial quiet time is. You must set aside time every day for quiet time with the Lord if you want to deepen your relationship with Him personally. It has been stated that quiet time is essential, but you may be asking yourself, "What is quiet time and why is it so important?"

The Importance of Spending Time in Silence with God

You intentionally schedule quiet time each day to be with God. You speak with God in prayer, and in quiet time, you receive His voice through His Word. Every human connection must grow and deepen by time spent with one another.

In the same spirit, spending time in prayer and reading God's Word is necessary to fortify and enhance your relationship with Him. God longs for you to share your entire being with Him in prayer and to open yourself to Him. You can discuss anything on your mind with Him.

God wants to know about every emotion you experience, including tension, anxiety, joy, sadness, and loneliness. 1 Peter 5:7 states, "Cast all your anxiety on him because he cares for you." God cares about you, so He wants you to give Him all of your problems.

He knows we are helpless without Him, therefore He takes great delight in solving our troubles and giving us peace of mind. During quiet time, we can speak with our Lord and Savior in a peaceful manner. During quiet time, we are welcome to sit at

Jesus' feet and listen to Him quote from the Bible. Jesus says that we must abide in Him in order to yield fruit for His Name (John 15:1-4).

When we routinely read God's Word and spend time in prayer, we are dwelling in Christ and growing closer to Him. Quiet time is not a religious or customary practice. It is spending time in prayer and reading the Bible.

The objectives of quiet time are to deepen our connection with Christ, increase our knowledge of Him, and grow closer to Him. If we neglect our alone time with the Lord, we will find ourselves on a path full of pain, loneliness, and despair. Our need for a relationship with God was inherent in our creation.

If we consistently neglect to read the Bible and pray to God, we will cause a split in our relationship with Him. The Lord did not create the gulf; rather, it was brought about by our own lack of quiet time, which has allowed us to stray from the Lord and would ultimately generate a gulf in our connection. Spending quiet time with the Lord includes reading the Bible, praying, and thinking back on your lessons.

It is a spiritual discipline to meet with the Lord in quiet time each day, but as with any discipline, there are major benefits to constancy in your quiet time with the Lord. Maintaining God as the focal point of our day, growing in self-control, and becoming more like Christ are all facilitated by consistently having our quiet time. These benefits are but a handful.

How to Make Time for God in Silence

There are a few things you should do to prepare yourself for quiet time with the Lord. The first step is to decide what is the best time of day for your quiet time. This could happen during the day, at lunchtime, or at night. You are free to select a time that works best for you, even though most people spend quiet time in the morning with the Lord. As the Bible tells us in Psalm 55:17, "Evening, morning, and noon I cry out in distress, and he hears my voice," we can be confident that God is always listening to us. Maybe you perform at your best early in the morning while most people are still asleep. Maybe after lunch in the afternoon would be a better time. Alternatively, it might be best for you right before bed.

Regardless of what you choose, make sure you schedule a certain period of time each day to have quiet conversations with the Lord. Secondly, determine the best location for your quiet time (Ibid.). Some prefer to relax at their kitchen table, while others would rather curl up in their favourite recliner.

You might even spend some quiet time in your garden if you discover that being outside helps you focus. Whether it's indoors or outdoors, make sure the setting you select will enable you to keep your full focus on the Lord. Steer clear of places that could distract you from your task, such as sitting in front of your computer with a ton of business emails coming in, visiting a busy coffee shop, or driving down the interstate.

Choose a place where you can focus properly and give the Lord your undivided attention. You could even name a room as your "quiet time room" and use it only for that purpose, if you're really creative. As a result, people will understand not to bother you when you are in your quiet time room.

Make sure the place where you spend your quiet time allows you to stay focused on the Lord. Lastly, you need to decide how long you want to spend in silence (Ibid.). You can spend fifteen minutes or longer in solitary time with the Lord.

After five to ten minutes of prayer, you might choose to spend the next five to ten minutes reading a chapter from a selected book of the Bible. Next, be sure to schedule some time to think back on the lessons you just learned from your meditation practice. Gradually increase the time you spend in the Lord's presence. As you learn to know Him better, you'll want to spend more time with Him.

What More Do I Require?

You will need a Bible, a ready heart, and perhaps a devotional book if you choose to read through one during quiet time. You can adopt a Bible reading plan or begin reading Genesis first and make your way through the entire text when you first start reading it.

Additionally, you could work on several Bible books under the direction of the Holy Spirit. Before you approach God in prayer, make sure your heart is in the right place. Don't just go into quiet time and start reciting prayers you've heard someone else say. Pray to the Lord in an honest, sincere, and transparent manner.

Think back on what you have learned after reading the Bible and praying to the Lord. Spend a few more minutes thinking over the lessons you have learnt and how you may use them in your day-to-day activities. The Bible is not designed to be skimmed hastily and then put away like a trash book.

It is intended that you study, comprehend, and apply the Bible to your everyday life. It is crucial to prioritise quiet time and should never be disregarded. While it is sometimes natural that you might be pressed for time, make sure you still set aside time for prayer and try to read at least a little portion of the Bible.

The Bible is the only means by which the Lord speaks to us in the modern era, and reading, studying, and reflecting on it is necessary if we are to receive His message. You will gain more knowledge about God, strengthen your relationship with Him, and develop into a more like Him person if you set aside time each day for quiet time.

You will yearn for daily quiet time with the Lord as your Christian life develops. Time with the Lord is sweeter than a few extra minutes of sleep, so you might even choose to get up early every day to spend more time in silence.

CHAPTER 9: PRAYER AND SPIRITUAL WARFARE

Recognizing Spiritual Battles

We must first admit that we are engaged in a fight before we can begin to comprehend the spiritual conflict. Smaller elements of the larger picture comprise battles. By definition, a battle is any kind of "extended contest, struggle, or controversy" that involves fighting between two people, between groups, or between armies (Webster-Merriam).Every day, as Christians, we engage in some kind of spiritual conflict. Battles are fought in warfare on various fronts, for various objectives, and to differing degrees of severity. It's the same with spiritual warfare. Despite the fact that we cannot see our attackers with our physical eyes, our spiritual struggles and combat are real. However, we may educate ourselves about the nature of the conflicts and how they affect our day-to-day lives.

We need to ask ourselves: "What makes us want to get involved in a spiritual battle at all?If we don't see a reason for the dispute, it won't help us to educate ourselves on it. Nowadays, there is a lot of debate concerning war in the actual world. These views, attitudes, and beliefs will carry over into the spiritual world. Regardless of our beliefs, there is a conflict occurring in the spiritual world. Either we are the winners or the losers. Jesus has arrived and triumphed. In the sky, the conflict is already won. Many of us enter into that covenant of salvation by grace, but Matthew 28:18 is not just about our salvation; it's also about our daily victory, which adds up to victorious living in Christ. Daily victory is achieved by knowing, believing, and understanding the battles that we are enduring on a daily basis, regardless of whether we are active or passive in the battles. Jesus told us in Matthew

28:18 that "All authority has been given to Me in heaven and on earth." We now have the privilege of having an eternal relationship with God.

Would you rather have all that God has in store for you here on earth now, or would you rather hold out for the benefits and victories until you reach heaven?

We will review and discuss what the Bible says regarding these areas and learn how to apply the scriptures to our personal lives to bring victory over these battles. We will examine three main areas of where the battles are fought: the Spiritual Battle, the Worldly Battle, and the Battle Within Us. It begins with learning the truth of God's Word and dispelling the lies of the enemy.

Spiritual Battle

Before we can discuss the spiritual battle, we must believe in the spiritual realm. We have a tendency to act like a two-year-old child who closes her eyes and places a blanket over her head, really believing that no one can see her because she cannot see them. Just because we cannot see the spiritual realm does not mean it is not there. Many believers and unbelievers today do not want to "deal" with a world we cannot see when the world we do see is hard enough to "deal" with.

Christian songwriter Keith Green once said, "I [Satan] used to have to sneak around. But now they just open their doors. No one's looking for my tricks because no one believes in me any more." Nevertheless, if we decide to reject or reject the spiritual realm, we will experience confusion, frustration, and a loss of the peace that God has promised to each of us. As they say, "the best defence is a strong offence." Knowing the spiritual realm is just half the battle, and God provides the other half of the fight.

Global Conflict

We have to believe in the spiritual realm before we can talk about the spiritual fight. We often behave like a two-year-old girl covering her head with a blanket and closing her eyes, truly thinking that nobody can see her since she is blind. The spiritual dimension does not cease to exist just because humans are unable to perceive it. The world we can see is difficult enough to "deal" with; a lot of believers and non-believers today do not want to "deal" with a world we cannot see.

"I [Satan] used to have to sneak around," Christian hymn composer Keith Green famously remarked. Now, though, they only open their doors. Nobody is searching for my techniques because they no longer have faith in me." However, if we choose to reject the spiritual world, we will lose the peace that God has promised to each of us along with uncertainty, irritation, and other negative emotions. "A strong attack makes for the best defence," as they say.

Understanding the spiritual world is only half the fight; the other half is supplied by God.

The Worldly Battle

People live in the world. Consequently, the way that humanity as a whole chose to live on Earth is referred to as the pattern of this world (Romans 12:2). As followers of Christ, we are instructed to live to please God, who exists outside of this world, rather than to follow the social conventions of others. In John 17:14–16, Jesus declared, "I have given them Your word; and because they are not of the world, just as I am not of the world, the world has hated them." I ask that You protect them from the wicked one rather than taking them out of this earth. They don't belong on this planet.

The Battle within us

Understanding what is happening in our own hearts and brains might be the most difficult and draining battle of all. This section will examine what the Bible says about the ongoing conflict between our physical and spiritual selves. Our members' "wars" with sin are what we fight. The most difficult spiritual warfare struggles that some of us face are internal ones. We are able to comprehend the conditions and events that the opponent employs in order to destroy us. We can concede that the world tempts and seduces us.

Preparing for the Spiritual War

Taking on Spiritual Conflicts in Jesus' Way

Jesus faced several different kinds of spiritual battle during His time on earth. For instance, the devil put Jesus to the test during His forty days in the desert (Luke 4:1–13). Those who disagreed with His teachings also verbally insulted, falsely accused, and provoked Him. Lastly, it is important to keep in mind that Jesus experienced all of the temptations that any other man would experience simply because he was a man—fully human.

What examples did Jesus provide us about using prayer to win the spiritual war? Even though He never lost a spiritual battle, His erroneous condemnation and crucifixion on the cross proved to be His greatest triumph.

Luke 5:16 (NIV) states that Jesus made space for God and Himself to be alone. "Jesus often withdrew to lonely places and prayed"

Throughout the Gospels, Jesus withdraws from what can be considered scenes of spiritual combat multiple times. For example, Jesus did not flee from His opponent when He heard that His cousin John the Baptist had been slain by Herod; instead, He withdrew from a certain area.

While praying while meandering around a park or coffee shop is totally fine, it's important to schedule regular time to be alone with God—ideally in an environment as devoid of distractions as possible.

How much more will it take for Jesus' followers to give God their whole attention and spend time with their heavenly Father if even Jesus, who is God, had to withdraw from the crowd and His associates in order to spend time alone with God.

God is always present and eager to spend time with us, healing our wounds and restoring our strength. Spending time in solitude with Him serves as a reminder of this.

PRAYING FOR SAFETY AND SUCCESS

SUCCESS

The bible says that we already have the victory: "Because everyone born of God triumphs over the world." This is the triumph that has triumphed over everything, including our faith." 1 John 5:4 (NIV) The definition of victory is defeating an adversary or resolving difficult issues.

So why do we still see so many Christians today leading defeated lives and never experiencing the fullness of joy that God has promised? The simple explanation is this: we are not using the power that God has given us! Being conscious of your power is one thing, but actually using it is quite another! How, therefore, can we use our power as God intended—that is, by walking in victory?

If we are to successfully use the authority God has given us and walk in victory, we must acknowledge and apply the following concepts.

QUINTET OF GUIDELINES FOR SUCCEEDING IN THE WIN:

1.The Connection Principle: Becoming a follower of Christ is a decision.

2. The Identity Principle: We can better remember our own identities if we have a genuine grasp of Jesus.

3. The Obedience Principle: We must be unwavering in our everyday endeavours to live in accordance with the teachings of the Bible.

4.The Fourth Fundamental Belief: God can always be trusted.

5. The Authority Principle: We must acknowledge that God is the source of our strength and power and maximise the authority he has given us.

Since Christ has set us free, it is hard to imagine that anybody would choose to live in defeat. Therefore, maintain your resolve and resist allowing yourself to once more fall under the yoke of slavery (Galatians 5:1, NIV). He has bestowed upon us a "New Authority"—the capacity to lead victorious lives—in this freedom. When we are unable to exercise the authority that God has given us, we eventually live in defeat, with a weakened spiritual life and a hollow purpose.

Since winning is the most exhilarating and happy thing there is, why should we endure a life of losing? In actuality, we have a choice: we can choose to live a life of failure, one that God did not pick for us, or we can accept the life of victory that God has already planned for us. I want to encourage you to take advantage of the newfound power God has given you and make the decision to live a victorious life!

We give thanks to God for sending His Son, Jesus Christ, to give us the victory!

Protection

God is ultimately the one who protects us. When faced with danger or spiritual or physical attack, those who place their trust in the Lord discover that He is an incredibly potent protector. The Bible says in Psalm 18:30, "He shields all who take refuge in him." Other scriptures that emphasise God's shielding presence are:

In the words of Psalm 32:7, "You are my hiding place; you will keep me safe from harm and envelop me in songs of deliverance."

"You give me a wide path for my feet so that my ankles do not give way; you make your saving help my shield, and your right hand sustains me; your help has made me great" (Psalm 18:35–36, emphasis added).

"You are my stronghold and protector; I have placed my trust in your promises" (Psalm 119:114, emphasis added).

However, you are my glory, my shield, and the one who holds my head high, Lord. "How numerous are my enemies, Lord! How many people rebel against me? (Psalm 3:1, 3).

Under the terms of the Old Covenant, God provided the Israelites with physical protection if they kept the law (Deuteronomy 7:11–26). Exodus 23:27, NASB) states that God also assured the Israelites that they would be secure from the countries who would oppose them once they arrived in the Promised Land. "I will send My terror ahead of you, and throw into confusion all the people among whom you come, and I will make all your enemies turn their backs to you." In this instance, God is standing up for people whose deeds were in accordance with His intended wills and desires

For those who fully rely on God, Psalm 121 is a wonderfully upbeat song. In Psalm 121:1-2, the poet declares that the source of his assistance is the Lord of all the world. He continues by teaching us about the Lord's constant watchfulness for His children, saying that the One who never sleeps is at work day and night (Psalm 121:3-6). Finally, the psalmist assures us that the God who is keeping watch over us will protect us and that He is ultimately in control of everything we do, both now and forever (Psalm 121:7-8).

Those who were aware of God's protection include Shadrach, Meshach, and Abednego (Daniel 3), Daniel (Daniel 6), Noah (Genesis7), David (Psalm 18:3; 54:7; 138:7), and Noah (Genesis 7). Job's life serves as another illustration of God's protection. Satan put Job through a lot during his tribulations, yet God placed boundaries that Satan could not breach; Satan could only do what God approved of and nothing more (Job 1-3). Job endured a great deal of pain and misfortune, but God was protecting him from worse. Furthermore, God preserved Job's confidence by permitting Job to undergo some testing prior to His intervention and communication with Job (Job 38–42). Job realised that even though he was unable to observe God at work in the background, God is dependable and trustworthy.

The ways in which God has provided for His people throughout Scripture demonstrate

His omnipotence and creativity: angels (Psalm 91:11–12), fire (2 Kings 1:9–10), floods (Judges 5:21), escape routes (Acts 9:24–25), royal decrees

(Ezra 6:11–12), heathen armies (Acts 23:23–24), and even sleeplessness (Esther 6).

God is able to free us from all material suffering, yet it could not be His will to do so. He sometimes purifies us via hardships. We ought to "count it pure joy" during these moments because, according to James 1:2–3, God allows difficulties to try our faith in order to make it stronger so that we can endure and become more like Christ. Therefore, we should not assume that God's promise of protection will spare us from suffering or loss. Job's narrative demonstrates this.

Furthermore, God does not always shield us from the bad effects of other people's misdeeds or the repercussions of our own transgressions because our world has fallen and we are vulnerable to suffering. Persecution is a common occurrence for many Christians (2 Timothy 3:12). Jesus gave His disciples assurance, saying, "I have revealed these things to you so that you may have peace in me. This world will be difficult for you. But be encouraged! The world is no more over me, says John 16:33. However, God is still in charge of all circumstances, and the depth of our pain is limited. God won't let anything happen to us that we can't handle (1 Corinthians 10:13). According to Jeremiah 5:22 (NLT), God declares, "The waves may toss and roar, but they can never pass the boundaries I set."

Rather than focusing on the promise of physical security that comes with the New Covenant, we emphasise God's spiritual protection against the enemies of our souls. To protect our hearts and minds, God has given us His own peace (Philippians 4:7) and spiritual armour (Ephesians 6:10–18). The Holy Spirit's eternal indwelling forms the basis of God's protection (Ephesians 2:21–22). Paul said in his letter, "The Lord will deliver me from all wickedness and will

Even if the Romans could do their hardest, Paul was confident that "to be absent from the body [is] to be present with the Lord" (2 Corinthians 5:8). "Take me securely to his celestial realm. Glory to him forever and ever. Amen, says 2 Timothy 4:18.

According to Ephesians 1:13–14, the believer is set apart for the day of final glorification. Heaven is our home, and no matter what occurs in this world, we are safe spiritually there. "Happy is the one who trusts in the LORD, whose confidence is in him," Jeremiah 17:8 declares. They will resemble a tree that was planted by water and spreads its roots along a stream. Its leaves are permanently green, thus it does not fear heat. It always bears fruit and is unafraid of a year of drought." (Romans 8:28–39).

**Know about prayers yourself
174**

Chapter 10: The Fruits of Effective Prayer

What Constitutes Effective Prayer?

God is neither a particle of substance or a chemical compound that can be put through tests. God exists as a living creature. Because of this, the prayer is considered successful when it possesses the following three qualities:

To Pray Effectively, You Must Know

It takes an intimate, personal relationship with God via Jesus Christ to be able to pray effectively. Jesus began the model prayer when his disciples asked him how they should pray, saying, "Our Father in heaven, sanctified by your

name" (Matthew 6:9). Accordingly, prayer ought to have a relationship focus. It necessitates familiarity with the petitioner. Jesus said that one should not pray to make a show out of prayer. Instead, one ought to "enter your room, close the door, and offer prayers to your Father who is hidden away." According to Matthew 6:6, "And your Father who sees in secret will reward you."

To Pray Effectively, You Must Believe

Believe in God, said Jesus. I really tell you that whoever says to this mountain, "Be taken up and thrown into the sea," and has faith in his ability to bring his words to pass, will receive his wish fulfilled. So whatever you ask for in prayer, believe that you have received it, and it will be yours, is what I am telling you (Mark 11:22–24). Therefore, to pray, one must have trust that God can grant their desire. Here is where a word of caution is necessary. Jesus explains that one must pray in accordance with the Father's wishes in the model prayer. That is to say, that while you may really want a multimillion dollar mansion, it might not be God's intention for you to possess one. Thus, it is necessary to maintain a balance between a person's sincere prayer and God's will.

To Pray Effectively, You Must Obey

In order for your Father in heaven to pardon your transgressions, Jesus commanded, "whenever you stand praying, forgive, if you have anything against anyone" (Mark 11:25). "Confess your sins to one another and pray for one another, that you may be healed of your sins," advises James. A godly person's prayer has tremendous power since it is actively at work (James 5:16). Peter suggests that there may be obstacles to prayer. In order to prevent your prayers from being hampered, Peter advises husbands to "live with your wives in an understanding way, showing honour to the woman as a weaker vessel, since they are partakers with you of the grace of life" (1 Peter 3:7). What does all of this suggest? It implies that a person's prayers might not be heard if they are not leading an obedient life before the Lord. You cannot expect God to do a miracle in your life if you are living in disobedience. It is not mocking God. James did not claim that a rebellious person's prayers have a lot of power. Instead, the pious person's prayers do.

Acknowledging Responses to Prayer

According to Elder Richard G. Scott, God responds to our petitions in three ways:

He gives us confidence by saying "yes."

He responds negatively to avoid making a mistake.

He chooses not to respond in order to support us in developing our faith in Him and in taking accountability for using the knowledge we have gained to make our own decisions.

When the Spirit can reach your heart and mind, the Lord most often gives you tiny answers through the Spirit's promptings. He calls you to consider, put your faith into practice, and take action with gentle proddings from the Spirit.

You can experience the Holy Ghost's constant companionship by living in accordance with God's teachings and the teachings of His apostles and prophets. This is the finest approach to identify answers to your prayers.

The goal of prayer is to get access to spiritual realities. Scripture tells us time and time again that the Lord hears our petitions. This post is about acknowledging and receiving answers to our prayers.

I have experienced many answered prayers, much like many of you who are reading this post. [1] As a result, I am acquainted with how the spirit operates. To become more adept at identifying solutions, we need to gain experience and time. My own experiences indicate that most prayers are answered by the spirit's subtle workings.[2] Nevertheless, these delicate, gentle replies can be misunderstood.[3] The way to solve this issue is to cry out to the Lord for assistance, asking to know his purpose and steer clear of blunders. Take note of how the term "cry" is used[4]. If you believe that pleading with the Lord is a bit excessive, I advise you to thoroughly study the scriptures. According to the scriptures, the prophets would often go "crying unto the Lord" in order to receive answers to their petitions.

I think the Lord is eager to hear our petitions and to teach us His ways, but we must follow the law, which is the foundation for blessings.

Enhancing our capacity to see and accept answers to our prayers can be accomplished in a variety of ways. In order to facilitate connection between Heavenly Father and ourselves, I would like to propose the following concepts.

1. Trust in the words of the Lord regarding prayer.

"Be thou humble; and the Lord God shall lead you by the hand, and give you answer to your prayers" .

The Lord's perspective on prayer is made clear by this and numerous other scriptures. When we look to the Lord for a response, we make our attitude toward prayer clear. Are we prepared to incur the costs? Recall that believing implies making the decision to set aside our doubts.

2. To receive an answer to your prayers, you don't have to be flawless.

The main obstacle, in my opinion, that prevents us from achieving goal number one is our tendency to become fixated on the notion that we must improve in order to receive a response from the Lord. We will easily forget about our "worthiness" and beg the Lord for what we need if our need is high enough. Nevertheless, if our need isn't the greatest, a lot of us will give up after a short while, thinking to ourselves, "The Lord won't answer my prayers because _____" (fill in the blank). Usually, we fill up the space with some sin that we unearth. This, in my view, is an indication of our spiritual anaemia.

3. Be tenacious in your pursuit of a spiritual solution.

Occasionally, a prayer is answered before we have completed it. However, we must wait on the Lord most of the time. Waiting on the Lord requires work; it is not a passive activity. diligence in both asking questions and exercising patience. "Were we to receive inspired guidance just for the asking, we would become weak," as Elder Richard G. Scott once stated[5]. In my opinion, a lot of churchgoers do not pray with patience and persistence. They get into the routine of expressing their heart's aspirations in prayer a few times and then moving on with the mindset that "whatever happens must be the Lord's will."

I would like to propose a method of pursuing a blessing that demonstrates patience and diligence in requesting. The Book of Mormon instructs us to offer three times a day for prayer. This suggests, in my opinion, that we should set aside some time, even if it's just a few minutes, to formally kneel before the Lord and make our requests known. We must assess our emotions once we've done this for a while. Have you sensed any encouragement from the Lord in your prayers? If so, keep going until you have a response. For more than 350 days, I prayed three times a day, every day, for a blessing. I began in early March, and almost a year later, in February, my request was answered. My inner conviction that the topics of my prayers were acceptable to the Lord was the only reason I persisted in requesting for so long. I found it entertaining and simple to pray for my desires. The solution appeared in a dream.

Consider fasting if, after a while of prayer, you experience no change. Ask the Lord for assistance. This takes us to the fourth number.

4. Take all the necessary actions to get the blessing you desire.

The Book of Mormon prophets approached the Lord by fasting and "crying unto the Lord"[6] for their deepest desires.[7] This gets us to number 5.

5. Observe and pay attention.

Sometimes the Lord may answer your request with something you need to accomplish first. Perhaps you need to confess something, perhaps you need to make amends to someone, or perhaps you need to persevere through a difficult time. It's critical to pay attention to your sensations and thoughts. That's why keeping a journal is crucial. Make a note of your feelings and thoughts, then act on them. I've discovered that my finest periods for inspiration come first thing in the morning, either as I'm waking up or right after, when my mind is clear.

A look out for "packets of help" These can take many different shapes, but they typically arise from outside assistance or involvement. Be alert; keep an eye out for coincidences, incidental encounters, and remarks you could hear from unanticipated people. The Lord answers our prayers in a variety of ways.

6. Study and read the scriptures, Ensign Magazine, and publications regarding prayer.

The readers of the Book of Mormon learn how to pray from it. I advise reading the Book of Mormon and researching the subject of prayer. This can be done by searching for terms and phrases associated with prayer on a computer.

I get great pleasure from reading about the answers to prayers. Latter-Day Voices, previously the Mormon Journal, is a section published in the Ensign magazine where members share their unique experiences with the Lord. Reading about these encounters strengthens one's faith.

"Receiving Answers to Our Prayers," written by Gene R. Cook is my favourite prayer book.

7. Accept the Holy Ghost as your travel partner as you endeavour to learn about God and His Son, Jesus Christ.

This is the most significant thing for which we can pray. Even though we always have urgent demands due to our mortality, there comes a point when each of us must prioritise the Lord and make a sincere effort to get to know Him.

GOING THROUGH A TRANSFORMATION

The definition of metamorphosis, according to the Cambridge English Dictionary, is "a change in something or someone's appearance or character, especially so that that thing or person is improved."

So what does a reformed life entail? A better life than one that has been transformed is a transformed life. A better Christian is one who has undergone transformation. Keep in mind that transformation is a process in which we are involved. I believe that we can have a significant impact on our own change if we are instructed to work out our salvation while shaking and afraid. You will know, and the world will know, when you have truly changed. People in your immediate vicinity will notice and recognize your transformation. Your parents, friends, and neighbours will all be aware of it. You can't change for very long; eventually, it will become apparent.

How to go about a life that has been transformed.

As a result, we should take note of the fact that we are transformed by the renewing of our minds, and the -ing at the end of renew implies that we must continually renew our minds. Romans 12:2 states that we should not conform to this world but rather be converted by the renewing of our minds. It ought to be a daily activity since a changed life begins with a renewed mind.

How does transformation come to be experienced every day?

Feed your mind with the word of God: read your bible, listen to inspirational music, watch preaching videos, and surround yourself with others who encourage you.

We should set our hearts on the things of heaven rather than the things of the world, according to Colossians 3:2. According to Matthew 6:21, your heart's desires will be fulfilled where your treasure is. Because we are aware that this world is not our permanent home and that we shall all eventually depart, having a heavenly mentality enables us to lead transformed lives. It is preferable to hoard treasures in heaven so that they will be there to greet you should you find yourself there at any point.

Avoid having a sexual mindset. Carnally mindedness is synonymous with death, according to Romans 8:6. Living a self-centered life where you don't give a damn about how your activities affect other people is a sign that you are carnally oriented.

Live a life full of the Holy Spirit. Tune yourself into the Holy Spirit. Since darkness and light cannot coexist, the holy spirit gives us guidance and light. Being in tune with the holy spirit means that you have no teacher, counsellor, comforter, or companion—you are just lost. The holy spirit is our teacher, comforter, and companion.

a life spent in adoration and gratitude since these things draw God's presence. He lives in people's admiration. "Cast me not away from thy presence, oh Lord," is what we see David saying to God. David understood the consequences of not having a right spirit and of not being in God's presence.

What is life that has been transformed?

It's found in Ephesians 6:13–18.

A transformed life dons all of God's armour in order to withstand the wicked day and come out unscathed. Regarding the dark day, it will arrive, but we are meant to resist it, and the only way we can do so is by donning all of God's gear.

A life of righteousness and truth is a transformed existence. We have to feel at ease speaking the truth. Truth belt: Just as belts keep our pants in place, truth belts keep our life in place. In the past, fighters' chests were shielded by breastplates, which are symbolic of righteousness. Righteousness shields us from the enemy's camp's swords and bullets while sin exposes us to them.

A changed life attracts people and shares the message. As Christians, we must mature to the point where we are at ease sharing the gospel and winning people over to the kingdom. Per the Bible, a wise person is one who wins souls.

A life that has been transformed is one filled with faith, which smothers the wicked's flaming darts. Faith asserts that Jehovah is my anchor, even in the face of death, adversity, and adversity in life. Keep in mind that hearing is the path to faith, so choose your listeners carefully.

A saved life, or a life of salvation, is a transformed life. A changed life also walks with the sword of the spirit, which is the word of God. God's holy word contains his will for our life; in order to stay transformed, we must read it and heed its instructions.

A life dedicated to prayer and intercession is a transformed life. You must make an investment in prayer and load your prayer bank. There will come a moment when you will not be able to pray, and nothing will keep you safe if your prayer bank is empty. Offer up prayers for yourself and those in your vicinity.

Advantages of leading a changed life.

Your life is imbued with a divine spirit and is supernatural. Living a supernatural life entails depending on God for guidance and fortitude. an existence apart from the natural.

Living a transformed life entitles you to all of God's blessings. God's benefits can often be wasted on us because we are not fully changed.

You lead a triumphant life, the life of a conqueror and an overcomer. The devil must not succeed in defeating us or take pleasure in our failure. We must get back up after falling so that God's name is exalted in our lives.

Testimonies to the faithfulness of God

Several examples show that God is loyal (see below). Numerous accounts of God's faithfulness may be found throughout the Bible, and individuals are constantly bearing witness today.

Reliability, constancy, and unwavering faithfulness are some of my favourite attributes of God. Dictionary.com defines faithfulness as "loyal, constant, and steadfast."

Scripture texts pertaining to God's faithfulness

The Bible is full of tales that support one another in conveying the idea that God is a reliable source. God has always been able to supply. Remember the promises He maintained for the Israelites. or the manner in which he extracted Daniel from the lion's den? God did not falter in the face of the Israelites' disloyalty, as the Bible makes clear.

Exodus 34:6: The Lord, the patient, kind, and kind God, full of unfailing love and faithfulness.

Knowing the Lord as God—the obedient God who upholds a covenant and steadfast love with those who love Him and obey His commands—is what Deuteronomy 7:9 teaches us.

Psalm 91:4: His loyalty is a buckler and a shield; He will cover you with His pinions and give you shelter beneath His wings.

1 Corinthians 1:9 says of God, "He who invited you to join Him in the fellowship of His Son, Jesus Christ, our Lord, is loyal."

2:13 - He still has confidence in us despite our adultery.

2 Thessalonians 3:3 says that the Lord is trustworthy. He will establish you and keep the evil one at bay.

Looking over this compilation of Bible verses makes me feel as though I'm in awe of the Lord. It reminds us of the true kindness and compassion that our Heavenly Father extends to those who trust in Him. God promises us that He won't leave us.

There are stories in the Bible about God's faithfulness.

Abraham and Sarah

Sarah was growing older and had no desire to become pregnant. She had been infertile her entire life until one day God spoke to her through a dream that she would become pregnant and bear a son called Isaac, who would start the Jesus family (Hebrews 11:11). What the Lord had promised was given to Sarah. And He most definitely kept His word. And from their newborn were born "offspring as numerous as the stars of heaven".

God's summons to the Israelites and Moses to go from Egypt paved the path for God to free them from slavery and take them to the promised land. This story will show you that God not only provides for the security of His people, but also utilises them to fulfil His promises. God uses people like YOU and me to carry out His will. He purposefully and intentionally created each of us. Even with Moses' speech handicap, God's people may be set free from servitude.

Furthermore, God would never desert you, unlike how He treated Moses during his difficult journey. He split the Red Sea to let the Israelites escape. He led them also in the Promised Land. It is clear that He gave the Israelites water and sustenance when they were in the desert. God consistently provides for His people.

Three Steps to Think About God's Faithfulness

When we think of God's faithfulness, it becomes evident to us that He always acts in the best interests of those who put their trust in Him. We have faith that He will deliver us from our difficulties, even though it may not seem like it when we are going through them. How much more will God supply for all of your needs if He can care for sparrows?

Read the Bible from cover to cover.

If you read the Bible, you will find that it is filled with stories of God's faithfulness. God is given a millennium of fidelity. It never ends and is limitless. The stories stated above, along with the life, death, and resurrection of Jesus Christ, show that God is dependable and that His promises will come to pass. How come God, who worked for those individuals, wouldn't work for our good as well?

Write down the Scriptures.

It can be difficult to remember God's faithfulness when things are difficult. Writing down the Scriptures helps bolster and reinforce your belief in

God. You can also list the prayers you've prayed and the times God has been true to you in your own life. By reviewing your previous encounters with God, you may come to feel even more certain that He is in control and always has your best interests at heart. It will also be a useful reminder that you are capable of overcoming obstacles.

Offer Up Your Prayers for Reliability

God will answer your prayers if you pray to Him. Trust that this is true, but also trust that God will bring about the desired outcome in His own time. When we pray to God and remind ourselves of our forgotten hearts, we will increase our faith and confidence in Him. Even though He doesn't always grant your desires, God always provides for your needs. He provides for us. God can't fail in keeping his words.

The next time adversity strikes, remember God's faithfulness by going through one of the previously listed procedures. Remind your heart of His faithfulness every day. We will never be able to honour Him completely. No matter what you're going through, you'll be able to put your trust in Him and experience hope restored. God alone offers us comfort, hope, treasure, and the knowledge that we will prevail!

CONCLUSION

I wanted to leave you with some closing thoughts and words of encouragement as we come to the end of our journey into the heart of prayer. Think of this as our parting conversation, but believe me when I say that the path of prayer is an adventure that lasts a lifetime.

Motivation: You Embrace Greater Strength Than You Acknowledge

I want you to know that you're stronger than you may believe, first and foremost. Embracing the practice of prayer requires bravery and an open heart. Prayer is a great compass to use when navigating the unexpected turns that life throws at you. Recall the strength that got you this far, no matter what obstacles you face.

Concluding Remarks: Your Relationship with God is a Lovely Tapestry

Remember this when you end the book: your relationship with the divine is a magnificent, dynamic tapestry. Every prayer, every silent time, every obstacle you have overcome is a part of the artwork that is your spiritual path. Treasure the teachings, recognize your progress, and have faith that God is always there to meet you where you are.

Remaining Devoted to a Life of Prayer: Everyday Decision, Not a Final Goal

Finally, remember that maintaining a life of prayer is a daily decision rather than a goal. The words may come naturally to you on some days and seem trapped on others. It's alright. Remaining devoted entails being present, especially in the face of difficulty, and realising that every prayer is an important strand in the vast tapestry of your spiritual development.

Shutting the Book, Hitting the Heart: The Journey Goes On

Thus, dear friend, let this be a time of celebration and introspection as you shut this book. You've embraced the strength of faith, dug into the beauty of prayer, and examined the subtleties of connection. The voyage does not finish here, though, and that is the true thing. It's only getting started, in fact. Even if the book is closing, your heart is still open to all the miracles that are still to come.

Remain devoted, maintain hope, and most of all, remain in touch. The divine is always prepared to have this lovely conversation with you. Your prayers matter, whether they are for ordinary needs, happy or sad situations. Both the cosmos and you care about them.

Appendix

Model Prayers

This appendix contains a number of sample prayers to help and inspire you on a variety of occasions. You are welcome to customise them, utilise them just as they are, or let them inspire you as you set off on your own prayer journey.

1. Morning Prayer:

Greetings, Creator

I give thanks with my heart when the sun rises. I am grateful for the gift of a fresh day. May your knowledge influence my choices and your light lead the way. Assist me in spreading your love throughout the globe today, and may I serve as an example of compassion and empathy. Indeed.

2. Prayer for Healing:

Kind Healer,

I come to you for comfort when I'm hurting. Put your consoling arms around the people who are experiencing pain. Bring their souls, minds, and bodies back to health. Give the caregivers courage, and may your serenity surround everyone in need like a comforting balm. Indeed

3. Appreciation for Dinners:

Rich Donor,

We give thanks for the meal that is in front of us as we assemble around this table. May this supper fuel our bodies and cultivate thankfulness in our hearts, and bless the hands that created it. Please remind us of those in need and motivate us to share your abundance. Indeed.

4. Advice on Making Decisions:

Astute Advisor,

At this life's crossroads, I look to you for direction. Light up my way with your knowledge. Give me the bravery to follow where you lead, and open my heart to hearing your will. May your kindness and grace be seen in every choice you make. Indeed.

5. Evening Thoughts:

Almighty Soother,

I consider the pleasures and difficulties of the day as it draws to an end. I'm grateful for the beautiful moments and the knowledge gained. Please give me restful sleep and let me sense your presence in my dreams. Keep a watch on my loved ones and grant us inner peace. Indeed.

Please feel free to modify these prayers to fit your own needs and preferences. Allow them to be the starting point for your personal dialogues with God, understanding that your distinct perspective and life experiences add richness to the prayer life.

Review page

Hello, Reader

I hope you are doing well as I write this! I'm contacting you because I value your viewpoint.I would be grateful if you could take a moment to discuss the book "[Book Title]," which I recently released. Your observations might offer insightful criticism and aid in the book's discovery for others.

Your review would be quite valuable, regardless of whether you thought it was great, had some helpful criticism, or anything in between. Sincere evaluations have a big influence and are essential for independent writers like me.

I sincerely appreciate your participation in this trip with me. Your assistance is greatly appreciated.

Best wishes

David J. Gouge

Printed in Great Britain
by Amazon

36716598R10119